Challenges in Primary Science

Challenges in Primary Science

Meeting the Needs of Able Young Scientists at Key Stage Two

David Coates and Helen Wilson

David Fulton Publishers
London

David Fulton Publishers Ltd
The Chiswick Centre, 414 Chiswick High Road, London W4 5TF

www.fultonpublishers.co.uk

David Fulton Publishers is a division of Granada Learning Limited, part of the Granada Media group.

First published 2003

10 9 8 7 6 5 4 3 2 1

British Library Cataloguing in Publication Data
A catalogue record for this book is available from the British Library.

ISBN 1 84312 013 5

Typeset by BookEns Ltd, Royston, Hertfordshire
Printed and bound in Great Britain by Thanet Press Limited, Margate, Kent

Contents

Acknowledgements

Our thanks go to our families for all their patience and support while we were writing this book. We are grateful to our colleagues at the Research Centre for Able Pupils, at Oxford Brookes University, for their friendship, expertise and encouragement. We want to thank Deborah Eyre who first gave us the opportunity to become involved in the field of gifted and talented education and who is both mentor and friend. We have also benefited greatly from our contacts with the many primary teachers with whom we have worked in recent years.

We are grateful to Brenda Keogh for permission to use the concept cartoon on p. 25.

1 Introduction

Science is all about thinking and questioning so it is a subject that is particularly suited for providing challenge for all children and especially the more able.

Gardner's (1993) study on seven 'creators of the modern era' includes the profound thought that creative individuals are those who see old knowledge in new ways and generate novel ideas or products in their domain. This is eminently true of the heroes of scientific thinking, such as Galileo or Einstein. Scientists need to be able to think creatively and deeply.

Diezmann and Watters (2000) make a comparison between evolutionary thinkers and revolutionary thinkers: 'Evolutionary thinkers build on and extend existing ideas and apply those ideas in new ways, while revolutionary thinkers are those creative geniuses who contribute ideas that lead to paradigm shifts.' This sums up beautifully the greatest scientists – they are the revolutionary thinkers. They are the ones who have had the courage to break away from the mould of the accepted thinking of their times. For a host of reasons, this type of thinking needs to be encouraged and nurtured.

The education of able pupils is a rapidly developing area. It can be argued that, in the long term, the consequences of developing children's scientific potential will have an impact at both a personal level and a national level, in relation to national competitiveness. These ideas are highlighted in the National Curriculum:

> Science stimulates and excites pupils' curiosity about phenomena and events in the world around them. Because science links direct practical experience with ideas, it can engage learners at many levels. Scientific method is about developing and evaluating explanations through experimental evidence and modelling. This is a spur to critical and creative thought. Through science, pupils understand how major scientific ideas contribute to technological change – impacting on industry, business and medicine and improving quality of life.
>
> (DfEE/QCA 1999)

When challenging the gifted and talented, it is not always necessary to look towards the amount of work that is done but rather to the cognitive demands that it makes upon children and, in particular, the use of higher order thinking skills. The need for such challenge is highlighted in Ofsted inspections of the provision for able pupils: 'To reach their full potential G & T pupils need challenging tasks that stretch them intellectually' (Ofsted 2000). Montgomery (1990) notes that,

> In order to achieve developmental differentiation it is necessary to redefine the central objectives in teaching as:
>
> - to enable the pupils to think efficiently, and
> - to communicate those thoughts succinctly, whatever subject content is under study.

It is salutary to pause and wonder if the weight of the curriculum in the primary school is such that there may be little time for the children to think hard because there is so much work to be done!

However, science teaching in the primary school need not fall into this trap. It can give children opportunities to extend their thought processes in some depth. We believe that it is possible to challenge children within science using the normal curriculum and activities that are commonplace in the primary classroom. The potential for challenge is there – it is a case of uncovering the cognitive curriculum.

Therefore, we argue that pupils' experience of primary school science should be exciting and be characterised by conceptual challenge, preparing them for the increased demands of the secondary school science curriculum. It is our contention that this more imaginative, creative and challenging approach will result in raised standards for the whole class. In support of this Mike Tomlinson, Director of Inspection at Easthamstead, Berkshire stated 'If schools are willing and able to meet the needs of able pupils, standards are raised for all pupils' (20 June 1995).

Identification

In the literature of different countries, many terms are used to describe the children for whom this work is aimed, for example 'able', 'highly able', 'gifted and talented'. The QCA *Guidance on Teaching Gifted and Talented Pupils* (2001a) defines gifted and talented as follows:

- Gifted pupils are those who have abilities in one or more subjects in the statutory school curriculum other than art and design, music and PE.
- Talented pupils as those who have abilities in art and design, music, PE, or in sports or performing arts such as dance or drama.

In our experience, teachers tend to be reluctant to describe a child as gifted and their natural inclination is to assume that this implies exceptional ability, such as that seen in Beethoven, Einstein or Picasso. Hence it is not unusual to hear the claim that 'There are no gifted children here.' However, the above definitions are norm-referenced, which means that the word 'ability' relates to the school population, and not the population as a whole. Therefore gifted pupils will be found in the majority of classrooms and in all schools. This book is designed to help meet the learning needs of such children.

Porter (1999) defines gifted young children as 'Those who have the capacity to learn at a pace and level of complexity that is significantly advanced of their age peers.' Maker (1982) suggests that gifted pupils differ from their classmates in three ways: the pace at which they learn, the depth of their understanding, and the interest they hold.

The current trend towards increased emphasis on literacy and numeracy, often to the detriment of science, may well contribute to the difficulty of identifying a pupil who is able within this particular subject. What then are the characteristics of a primary-aged pupil who is specifically gifted in science and are these different from those that would be exhibited in other subjects?

Of course some children are good all-rounders and are gifted in most subjects. However, we have personally met children in our teaching careers who are gifted in science but not necessarily in other areas. They have been articulate about their discoveries and have had an enthusiasm in science, which was far from evident in other subjects. One of these children was particularly memorable. He had a reputation as a 'naughty boy' whose behaviour often left much to be desired. He struggled with his English and mathematics and often ran out of patience. However, in science, if he was allowed to report his findings or express his understanding verbally, he could genuinely shine. His reply to the question at the end of the lesson, 'Who can tell me what they have learnt today?' was often staggering. This was obviously good for his self-esteem and it also showed a potential, which probably would not otherwise have been evident.

A child's lack of ability in literacy and numeracy may hinder their long-term progress in science, but this need not necessarily be the case at the primary level. Science is different and it is helpful to consider possible indicators of ability within this particular discipline.

Methods of identification

Both qualitative and quantitative data can be used for the identification of a pupil who is able in science. However, quantitative data alone, such as the use of Standard Assessment Tests (SATs), may result in some pupils being missed. Freeman (1998) highlights the need for identification processes to provide 'multiple opportunities, rather than multiple hurdles' so that all children can be given opportunities to maximise their potential.

Primary teachers tend to know their pupils well and teacher nomination has much to recommend it. However, care must be taken that this form of identification is evidence based and not purely subjective. Pupils' behaviour can sometimes influence judgements and also ability in science is not always linked to ability in literacy or numeracy.

Parental nomination can also be revealing, as parents possess information about their child's particular interests and passions. This type of information can be gained by an extra question during interviews at parents' evenings, such as 'What do you think are your child's particular interests or strengths?' Taking this further, Hymer and Michel (2002) have developed a questionnaire and a multiple intelligence profile for parents to provide valuable information about their child.

Self- and peer nomination also have potential and, if handled sensitively, can be a useful source of data. As children become more involved in their own learning, they are more aware of their own abilities and so may, for example, choose to nominate themselves for optional science activities. In terms of peer nomination, answers to questions, such as 'Who would you go to for help with your science?' can be revealing.

O'Brien (1998) emphasises the fact that the scientifically more able child does not just show good knowledge about science. Sometimes they use a vocabulary that is beyond other pupils of their age. They may ask perceptive, provocative questions and apply their background knowledge of the subject in an interesting way, making links in their understanding. They also may be intensely curious about science and become engrossed in ideas and investigations.

A checklist can be a useful tool to help teachers in this identification process and particularly can help to maintain the subject specificity. The specific characteristics of able primary children in relation to science, which we devised from our work with gifted children (Coates and Wilson 2001), may include some or all of the following:

- a natural curiosity about the world and the way things work
- an enjoyment of hypothesising
- an ability to express scientific knowledge and understanding logically and coherently
- scientific vocabulary used accurately and appropriately
- an ability to transfer knowledge and understanding from one situation to another
- an ability to spot and describe patterns in results
- innovation in experimental design and/or in the collecting and recording of data.

The QCA *Guidance on Teaching Gifted and Talented Pupils* (2001a) includes another extensive checklist of 23 characteristics, from which a range may be evident in scientifically gifted children.

However, there are obviously some limitations to any checklist. For example, they can indicate the type of giftedness but not the degree and they do not indicate how much of the criteria needs to be met to be considered gifted (Porter 1999). The QCA checklist is designed to be used with all children from Key Stage 1 to Key Stage 4. It is self-evident that children aged five will not exhibit the same characteristics as a more able 16-year-old.

Monitoring pupils' performance when faced with cognitive challenge in science is possibly the most powerful identification tool. This is identification through provision, which Freeman (1998) calls the sports model. The sports analogy is apposite because, in order to discover who is the best high jumper, the bar is raised for all and we watch to see who can make the leap. Therefore providing the whole class with challenging tasks and questions will result in opportunities for pupils to demonstrate the depth of their thinking and understanding. Once again, we can watch to see who makes the leap. The learning context is therefore seen to be an essential feature of this more flexible means of identification. Hence aptitude and provision are considered together to find and provide for potential strengths and abilities.

Identification therefore occurs when teachers recognise the advanced way in which a child responds to the curriculum. This method of teaching is a continuous and exciting process, which motivates the more able pupils and encourages them to identify themselves through their achievements. If this identification process does not rely solely on the pupils' literacy skills, this approach will also help to identify the vulnerable groups of more able pupils who may otherwise underachieve. If children are not given the opportunities to respond to cognitively challenging questions and activities, their true ability may never be uncovered.

Using the challenge strategies discussed in Chapter 2 should facilitate the identification of ability in science through challenging provision for all the pupils. The range of identification tools taken together will provide a fuller picture of ability as shown in Figure 1.1. A deeper understanding of the pupils' ability will then feedback into the planning of appropriate provision.

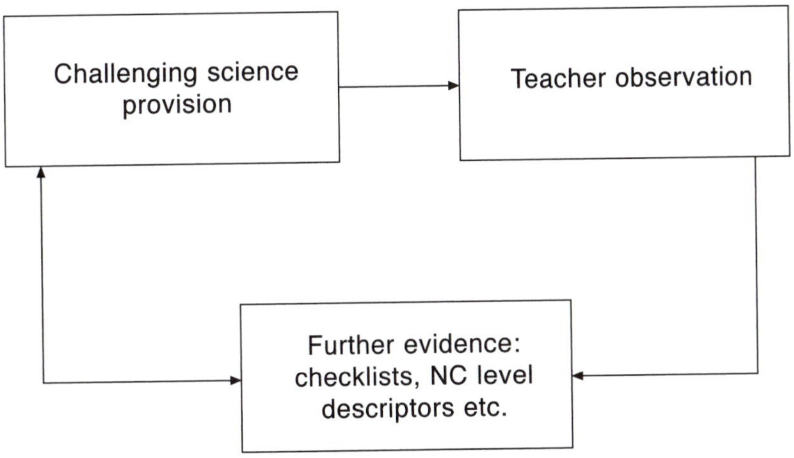

Figure 1.1 Identification of ability in science through provision

Why bother?

In light of the great burdens already placed on primary teachers, why add to this by introducing a need to identify able children within individual subjects? Identification of able children only makes sense when it is linked to effective provision and this, in turn, is linked to the individual child's rights. George (1997) states that:

> Educationalists are agreed that it is every child's right to go as far and as fast as possible along every dimension of the school curriculum in order to reach their considerable potential, and that this is one of the main aims of education.

All children surely have a right not to be bored but to be excited by their learning.

However, do gifted children merit special attention? Surely gifted pupils can achieve highly without significant support from their teacher? Eyre (1997) notes that it was a commonly held belief that able children would always be successful, regardless of their circumstances, but that this has been disproved. Eyre states that research, such as that done by Freeman (1991), in her account of gifted children growing up, indicates that support and encouragement are vital to success.

This has also been highlighted in a recent white paper:

> Too often in the past, the most able have not got the targeted support they need. There has sometimes been a reluctance to recognise their particular needs and a feeling that they will do well anyway. In the past, too many of our able children have not done as well as they should.
>
> (DfES 2002)

Gagné (1991 cited in Davis and Rimm 1998), working in Canada, notes that catalysts, such as environmental, intrapersonal and motivational, are needed to transform a person's intellectual abilities into academic performance. Renzulli (1986) states that pupils need a combination of innate ability, creativity and task commitment before they can truly demonstrate their giftedness. Eyre (1997) has summed these ideas up in the model:

Ability + Opportunity/Support + Motivation = Achievement

Within this model, science is an ideal subject to provide motivation in the primary school because it is 'different' and it should be obviously different from any other subject. The provision of suitable opportunities and support is the challenge facing the primary teacher.

Challenge and gifted scientists

The challenge then for a primary teacher is to plan for a working environment in which all pupils, including the most able, can fully develop their capability and interests within a normal mixed ability class. This obviously requires careful planning but it is important to note here that provision for the gifted does not need to result in a fourth layer of differentiation. The advantage of provision for the gifted is that it builds on existing good practice and it involves doing what is done anyway but hopefully, 'doing it even better'.

Science teaching needs to be differentiated, to allow for the needs of gifted and talented pupils, by task, inputs and outputs, for example through a range of learning outcomes. In the guidance for working with gifted and talented children (QCA 2001b) within the numeracy and literacy strategies five key dimensions are highlighted for the planning of appropriate differentiation:

- breadth
- depth
- acceleration
- independence
- reflection

These five key dimensions pertain equally well to primary science lessons and will be addressed in turn.

Breadth

Breadth involves 'going sideways', beyond the confines of the science National Curriculum, but not necessarily at a greater level of complexity. For example, the Earth and Beyond section of the science National Curriculum at Key Stage 2 requires that pupils should learn about the Earth, Moon and Sun. There is no mention of the other planets so work can be embarked upon which focuses on the other members of the Solar System. If planned imaginatively, this will create considerable interest for the pupils and add to their sense of the awe and wonder within science.

Depth

Depth involves an increase in the complexity of the task but without going beyond the actual content of the normal curriculum. This will often involve the encouragement of the pupils to access higher order thinking skills (Bloom 1956), which will be discussed in more detail later. Science lends itself particularly well to this type of challenge. For example, it is a requirement of the Key Stage 2 science curriculum that pupils learn that the Earth spins on its own axis and travels around the Sun. When this motion is acted out, the pupil who takes the role of the Earth soon becomes dizzy. This begs the question, 'Why do we not feel dizzy?' Hopefully, this will require the pupils to think in depth and, most importantly, to enjoy postulating and discussing. This example is given in Chapter 7.

Acceleration

Acceleration involves covering the material more quickly and embarking on work from the following key stage. The children are accelerated through the curriculum and this may result in some primary age children being taught parts of the secondary school syllabus.

Acceleration as a way of creating sufficient challenge for highly able children can be a particular problem for primary teachers, especially in areas of the curriculum where they lack confidence or specific expertise. It will inevitably result in overlap with work that pupils will be doing in later years and it can be demotivating for pupils to repeat work. However, it may be appropriate in certain areas of the curriculum. For example, if the electricity section of the science curriculum is delivered through a technique of structured discovery learning, some pupils will progress very quickly and will discover parallel circuits. However, there is no need for a detailed explanation of the working of these circuits, beyond the mention that they are 'special cases' that they will meet later in their school career.

Independence

The more able pupils can be encouraged to plan and carry out investigations with less adult support than the rest of the class. Pupil research can also be a useful tool for challenge, as long as it is not a case of pupils being completely left to their own devices, with no structure or planning behind the exercise. It is possible to link this back to the previous examples from the Earth and beyond section of the Key Stage 2 syllabus. Pupils' research on other planets in the Solar System can be undertaken independently, by allowing them access to the Internet, CD-ROMs, books etc. The focus and depth of research can be increased by asking them to use the acquired information to prepare a four-minute 'foreign correspondent's report' from that planet. They will need to mention how they feel, what they can see in the sky, how they are managing to breathe etc. and their reports can be recorded on an audio tape. This example is given in Chapter 7.

Reflection

This involves making explicit what they understand and evaluating what they have done. Evaluation is the final stage of an investigation and is an integral part of scientific enquiry but it is something that is too easily omitted because of time constraints. It gives pupils the opportunity to learn to criticise their work and suggest improvements. In the previous example of the foreign correspondent's report, reflection can involve the pupils listening to their taped reports and suggesting and implementing alterations of style, content etc.

The publication *Investigations: Developing understanding* (Goldsworthy *et al.* 2000a) encourages reflection and evaluation of other pupils' opinions and ideas. As these 'other pupils' are fictitious, it has the advantage of allowing criticism without pain. It can be fun to pick holes in others' work but it can also be instructive when improvements are suggested. The book is aimed at the Key Stage 2/3 transition phase and is therefore ideal for challenging able children in upper primary.

Thinking skills

> Higher order thinking occurs when a person takes new information and information stored in memory and interrelates and/or rearranges

> and extends this information to achieve a purpose or find possible answers in perplexing situations.
>
> (Lewis and Smith 1993)

This definition of higher order thinking is both interesting and pragmatic. In today's information-rich society, surely education should encourage individuals to develop the necessary skills to process and evaluate material – to do something with it! Life is often full of 'perplexing situations' and so it can be argued that the value of this type of thinking should go far beyond the National Curriculum. Thinking is a tool for life.

Bloom (1956) designed the following taxonomy as a guide for writing learning objectives. It draws attention to the difference between low level knowledge, which is commonly taught and high level thinking which is taught less often (Davis and Rimm 1998). It is therefore important to plan a curriculum that includes thinking skills. Bloom describes six levels of thinking arranged hierarchically in order of complexity, with the last three being considered as higher level:

- **Knowledge**: remembering previously learned material
- **Comprehension**: ability to grasp the meaning of material and convey it to others
- **Application**: ability to use learned material in new contexts or situations
- **Analysis**: ability to break down data into significant component parts
- **Synthesis**: ability to create new structures using combinations of learned parts
- **Evaluation**: ability to judge material in terms of its value for a given purpose.

However, seeing thinking skills as a hierarchy is not always helpful. Commonly now Bloom's higher levels of synthesis and evaluation are categorised as critical and creative thinking. In simple terms, evaluation might be considered equivalent to critical thinking and synthesis equivalent to creative thinking, and both require analysis of ideas. McGuinness (2000) has listed the characteristics, which are associated with critical and creative thinking in more detail:

- Critical thinking skills: making predictions, hypothesising, drawing conclusions, justifying conclusions, distinguishing fact from opinion, determining bias, checking the reliability of evidence, relating cause and effect.
- Creative thinking skills: generating new ideas, brainstorming, formulating own points of view, combining ideas, recognising and using analogues.

There are obviously close links between these ideas and the science curriculum. Indeed the terms scientific method, science process skills and critical thinking are sometimes used to denote the same thing. Bloom's taxonomy is therefore a useful way of describing different types of thinking, but it seems more appropriate and pragmatic to divide it simply into higher and lower order thinking.

As teachers, we surely want children to learn meaningfully, to think flexibly and to make reasoned judgements. Therefore we are not simply concerned with the mastery of basic facts. A broader range of competencies, which can be defined as higher order thinking skills, need to be developed if we are to achieve these goals. The assumption is that thinking goes beyond the acquisition of knowledge and includes the processing of the information and reflection on the thinking involved (metacognition).

The teaching of these lower *and* higher order skills should be closely interwoven in the classroom (Lewis and Smith 1993). While lower and higher order thinking may be taught together in a class, for a given individual the need to use higher order thinking will depend upon the nature of the task and the person's intellectual history. It can be argued that gifted children should be allowed to spend more time on higher level activities (Davis and Rimm 1998). Overt encouragement of the use of higher order thinking skills is often the key to effective differentiation for gifted pupils.

Shore (2000) has carried out research into gifted children's thinking and learning and concluded that they use strategies others do not use. These strategies include a three-way interaction between speed, flexibility and metacognitive ability. Allebone (1998) identified one of the characteristics of able children as their ability to use higher order thinking skills at an earlier age.

The human brain's capacity for higher order thinking skills is developed when myelination (the development of myelin, a fatty material forming an insulating jacket around a nerve fibre) takes place: this improves the connection between cells (Cheshire County Council 2002). This process of building connections in the brain begins at birth and is advanced and stimulated by the child's interactions with his/her carers. The most intense time for the development of these pathways in the brain is in the child's early years. However, the process never stops and current research in brain scanning suggests that the best way for able pupils to develop the myelination process is to encourage higher order thinking skills and to rehearse and practise these skills in a variety of contexts. Therefore it is the teacher's privilege to encourage the development of these connections in the brain.

Science and thinking skills

As has already been suggested, science is a subject that is particularly suitable for extending and deepening thinking. The famous scientist, William Lawrence Bragg said: 'The important thing in science is not so much to obtain new facts as to discover new ways of thinking about them' (cited in Mackay 1977). However, in order to achieve this it is crucial to depart from the impression that science is an illusive quest for the 'right' answer – and to become aware that it is a huge and amazing subject.

Thinking skills for all children are key elements in the National Curriculum and their importance is summarised by QCA/DfEE (2000): 'By using thinking skills children can focus on knowing how as well as knowing what – on learning how to learn. Many aspects of science contribute to the development of thinking skills.' The *Science teacher's guide update* to the science Scheme of Work (QCA/DfEE 2000) gives guidance on different types of thinking including:

- **Information-processing skills**. These enable children to locate and collect relevant information, to sort, sequence, compare and contrast, and to analyse relationships.
- **Reasoning skills**. These enable children to give reasons for opinions and actions, to draw inferences and make deductions, to use language to explain what they think, and to make judgements and decisions informed by reasons and/or evidence.
- **Enquiry skills**. These enable children to ask relevant questions, to pose and define problems, to plan what to do and ways to research, to predict outcomes and anticipate consequences and to test conclusions and improve ideas.
- **Creative thinking skills**. These enable children to generate and extend ideas, to suggest hypotheses, to apply imagination, and to look for alternative outcomes.
- **Evaluation skills**. These enable children to evaluate information, to judge the value of what they read, hear and do, to develop criteria for judging the value of their own and other's work or ideas, and to have confidence in their judgements.

Science generally can provide many opportunities for higher level thinking, but recent Ofsted reports (Ofsted 1999) in England indicate that this is not always a routine outcome of classroom science. Luxford (1997) suggests that content-based teaching, which she describes as the focus of most primary science lessons, only deals with lower order thinking. There is an inherent danger that the focus of primary science lessons becomes the imparting of factual information, rather than an encouragement of thinking.

Science lessons provide an ideal framework for cognitive work and the use of higher order thinking skills. O'Brien (1998) notes that:

> Children reveal something of their close understanding of science and the way they are viewing the world in the way they tackle thinking problems. It is therefore important for teachers to observe closely the way pupils think in science as well as what knowledge they display.

O'Brien (1998), who is writing specifically with science in mind, goes on to state that the qualities that are desirable in children are:

- to be confident thinkers, clear about the means;
- the capacity to enjoy thinking and consider the beauty of the process rather than the chore of the operation;
- to consider concepts with care and not to dismiss them in haste;
- to trawl widely for ideas to encourage originality and creativity but to be on target with that breadth;
- to use the fine tools of thinking like a surgeon's knife for incisive conclusions.

This is an exciting list and sets out both the challenge and the potential for primary science. The encouragement for the children to draw on their higher order thinking skills will be a feature that runs throughout this book and underpins most of the suggested activities or tasks. The approach of incorporating thinking explicitly into an existing subject is called **infusion**. To infuse means 'to introduce into one thing a second thing which gives it extra life, vigour and new significance' (*Webster's Third New International Dictionary* 1981). By doing this we can match thinking skills directly to a science topic and develop teaching which leads to deeper understanding. The approach that is taken in this book can therefore be described as an infusion model.

Metacognition

Metacognition is thinking about thinking. Children need to be encouraged to think deeply and also to be aware of their own thought processes. Fisher (1990) indicates that successful thinking is determined by efficiency in the three operations of:

1. acquiring knowledge – input
2. strategies for using knowledge and solving problems – output
3. metacognition and decision making – executive control.

In this context, the first operation involves covering the content of the science National Curriculum and in the second operation children are utilising that knowledge. In the final stage, they are reflecting on their learning strategies and how and when they have used them. Figure 1.2 represents this three-tier process. This model shows the importance of the content as it forms the foundations for the higher order thinking involved in the other two operations.

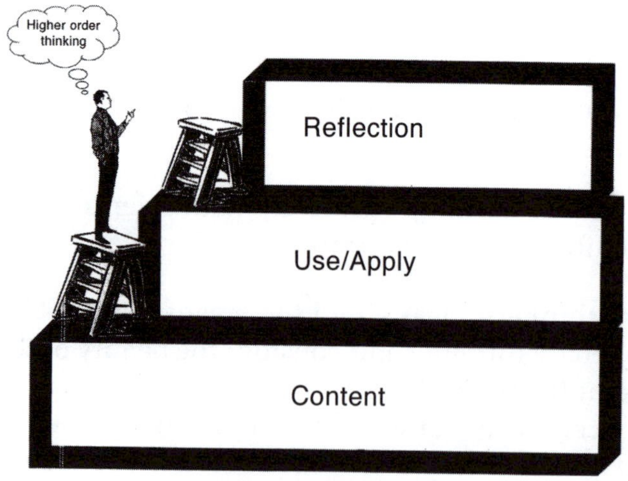

Figure 1.2 Developing successful thinking in science

Pupils can be encouraged to talk to each other and their teacher about how they solved problems. 'What were you thinking about when you did that? How did you get that answer?' Some teachers have introduced Bloom's (1956) taxonomy (discussed earlier in this chapter) to their pupils and encouraged them to consider which thought process they have accessed during the lesson. Whilst this is probably only suitable for the oldest children in primary schools, it has interesting possibilities.

Cognitive conflict

Cognitive conflict is what occurs when a person realises that their accepted understanding of a situation is directly challenged, does not hold true and so needs to be adapted. It takes children beyond their comfort zones to higher order thinking processes. Wood (1991) describes this as a state of conflict between what a child expects because of his or her interactions with the world and what actually transpires. Learners therefore, experience a puzzle or problem that poses a challenge. Any new information can only be interpreted by what we already know, have experienced or understand.

A key feature of teaching is to give children opportunities such as this to make connections between new learning and things that are familiar to them. If no connections are made, no learning takes place. 'The mismatch between new learning and the learner's existing store of experiences results in cognitive conflict' (Cheshire County Council 2002). In many ways, this process lies at the very heart of scientific thought, as the laws of science are constantly tested and reassessed.

Cognitive conflict can be used to challenge and then take forward children's thinking in a variety of ways. Asking children to hypothesise about the outcome of an investigation or experiment can introduce such conflict if the outcome is unexpected. For example, many people will think that a coat on a snowman will cause him to melt more quickly because coats keep us warm (see cartoon in Figure 2.3, Naylor and Keogh 2000). An investigation which models this scenario will show that this is not the case. Once this has been demonstrated practically, the pupils can be encouraged to readjust their thinking about this problem. In fact, the coat acts as an insulator and slows down the melting process.

Risk taking

Able children benefit from a challenging environment where they can take risks, even sometimes to the point of failure. A good question to ask in terms of provision for able pupils is whether or not they are sometimes challenged to the edge of their ability. A challenging curriculum will, at times, require significant effort to master and may take pupils beyond their normal comfort zone. This will result in the able pupils sometimes being wrong or not reaching the expected conclusion. This will then give them the opportunity to evaluate their thinking and hence learn to be more reflective, within a supportive and accepting environment.

The development of a supportive classroom ethos where pupils are encouraged to take risks will be central to the development of challenge. It will also be necessary for the pupils to understand that the deep thinking is more important than obtaining a correct answer. Surely a situation in which the able pupils are always 100 per cent correct is ultimately unhealthy? Lewis and Smith's (1993) definition of higher order thinking describes one of its functions as to find possible answers in perplexing situations. Life is full of perplexing situations and learning to cope with failure and to reflect and re-evaluate as a result of the experience is a life skill which should not be denied to able pupils.

However, we are not in any way advocating the pressurising or 'hot-housing' of the children but rather the creation of an atmosphere in which it is fun to learn and allowable to take risks. Csikszentmihalyi (1990) has presented an interesting model which relates challenge to skill levels (Figure 1.3). The vertical axis represents challenge and the horizontal axis the skill level. Where challenge is high and skills are low, there is frustration; where challenge is low and skills high, there is boredom. What we are aiming for is both high challenge and high skills and this results in what Csikszentmihalyi calls flow. Therefore expectations need to be high enough for individuals to experience challenge while skills levels need to be high enough for children to rise to that challenge and reflect on the outcomes, rather than flounder and feel depressed or worried.

Scaffolding the pupils' learning will play an important role in the development of a classroom ethos, in which children experience flow. This involves the provision of a variety of support strategies to extend pupils' cognitions (Rosenshine and Meisters 1992 cited in Diezmann and Watters 2000). The role of the teacher is crucial as she or he should not simply be setting the challenging

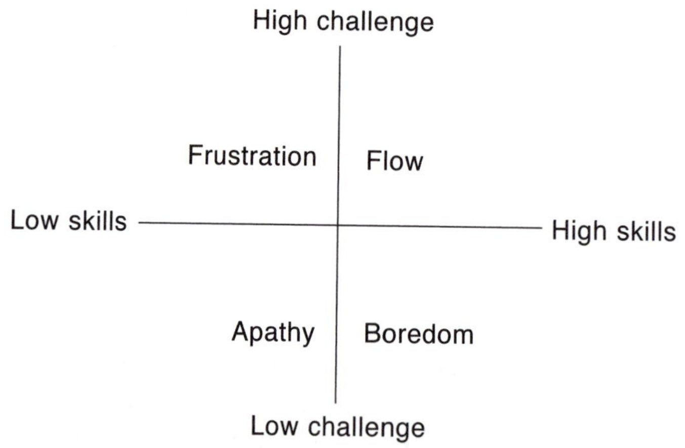

Figure 1.3 Model relating challenge to skill levels (Source: Csikszentmihalyi 1990)

task but should also be scaffolding the pupils in their development of scientific reasoning. What is needed to maximise the potential of activities is contact and time with the teacher. This is true for children of all abilities.

The science National Curriculum has immense potential for providing challenge and a focus on higher order thinking will result in what can be called 'an uncovering of the cognitive curriculum'. This will take the content of the curriculum and focus on or build upon the areas particularly suited for challenge. The emphasis will be on activities which develop critical and creative thinking linked to metacognition.

2 Planning for challenge

Scientifically gifted pupils can be catered for through differentiating the curriculum as part of the normal classroom organisation. This does not require a fourth layer of differentiation. However, it is not simply the content and process of science that we need to concentrate on, but the excitement of scientific discovery as well.

Maker and Nielson (1995) make the point that the provision for gifted pupils should be 'qualitatively different' not more of the same. If, once they have finished a task, they are always given more work of the same type or yet another worksheet, able children soon realise that the intelligent thing to do is never to finish before anyone else. The skill of the teacher is to ensure that the differentiation is appropriate, effective and exciting so that the children are engaged in their learning.

It is essential to provide an extensive range of experiences and examples so that pupils' mastery of the important concepts embedded in the National Curriculum is strengthened (Gallagher 1985). The Center for Gifted Education at the College of William and Mary, in the USA, indicates that the essential features of a science curriculum that meets the needs of gifted children include an emphasis on:

- learning concepts
- higher level thinking
- enquiry, especially problem-based learning
- the use of technology as a learning tool
- learning the scientific process, using experimental design procedures.

(Van Tassel-Baska 1998)

It is our strong contention that the science National Curriculum provides material which is highly suited to providing this type of challenging diet. As we have said, the potential of the curriculum for such challenge merely needs uncovering and emphasising. This was summarised in the Government Education and Employment Committee report 'Highly able children': 'Highly able primary school children need to be sufficiently challenged. Partly, this will be achieved through appropriate teaching and expectation of pupils. But it can also be achieved through the curriculum' (House of Commons 1999).

Lesson planning usually links to the QCA Science Scheme of Work or the school's existing medium-term plan. Recent studies in America have identified materials that are most appropriate for challenging gifted children in primary schools and these proved to be similar in emphasis to the English National Curriculum (Johnson *et al.* 1995). These include a balance between process and content, an emphasis on original student investigations, concept development and interdisciplinary applications. If this vision of science is realised then it will be an exciting and challenging subject for all primary children.

Eyre (2002) used the interesting phrase, 'structured tinkering', to describe such processes as teachers participating in small-scale action research projects to investigate and facilitate effective provision for able pupils. It seems reasonable to apply this phrase to the uncovering of challenge in the science curriculum. Tinkering brings to mind the person who goes under the bonnet of a car to finely tune the engine. The car itself is a given and cannot be changed but it can be tuned to achieve maximum performance. Similarly, the science National Curriculum is a given but it too can be tuned for maximum performance. However, to tinker with a car engine requires some skills and so does the tuning of the curriculum. Some suggestions for this type of tinkering are given in this chapter. A list of resources which can help in the planning for challenge is given at the end of this chapter.

Figure 2.1 shows a model for the teaching of primary science in a way which is designed to provide challenge. Around the circle are four challenge

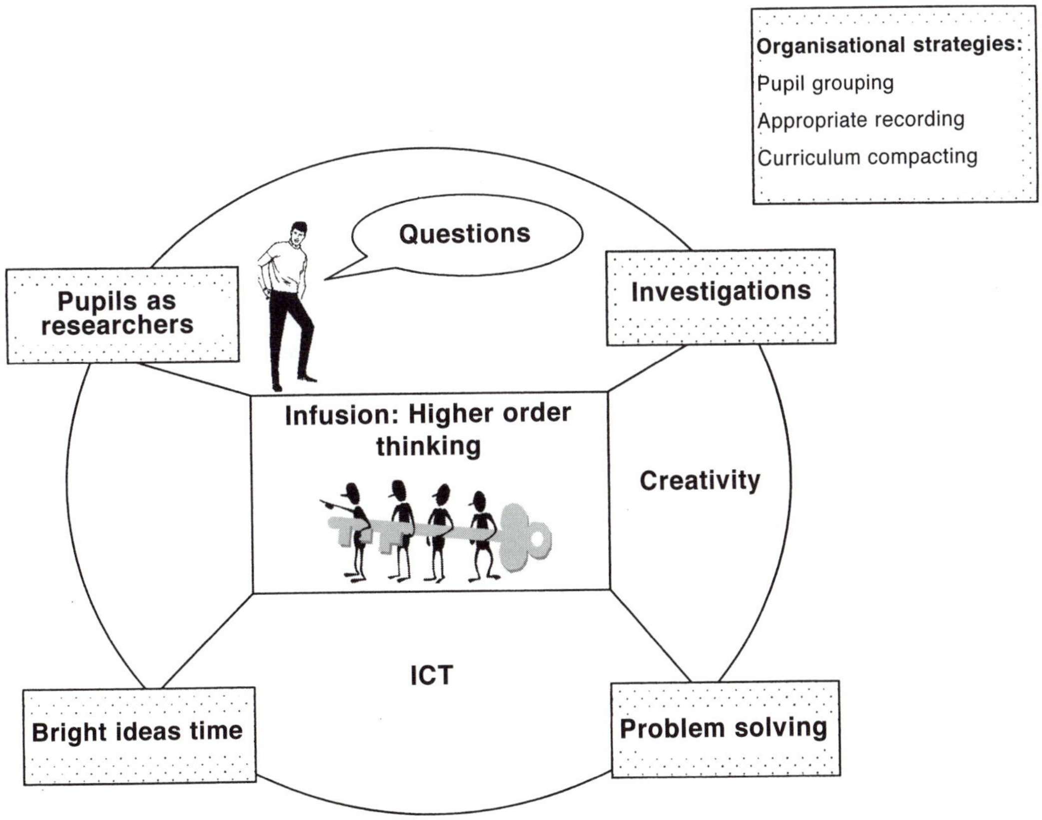

Figure 2.1 A model for teaching primary science to provide challenge

strategies, which can be planned into lessons to enhance the pupils' learning experience:

- Bright ideas time
- Pupils as researchers
- Problem solving
- Investigations.

Bright ideas time, pupils as researchers and problem solving will be addressed in turn and exemplified in this chapter. Investigations will be discussed in detail in Chapter 4, 'Scientific enquiry'. These challenge strategies in science lend themselves particularly well to ensuring appropriate differentiation within the five key dimensions of breadth, depth, acceleration, independence and reflection, which have already been discussed in Chapter 1. They also link to suggestions for enriching and extending pupils' experiences as set out in the QCA *Guidance for Teaching Gifted and Talented Pupils* (QCA 2001c: www.nc.uk.net/gt/science/index.htm) (see Table 2.1).

Table 2.1 QCA Guidance for Teaching Gifted and Talented Pupils – science (*Source:* QCA 2001c)

Challenge strategy	QCA guidance for enriching and extending pupils' experiences
Bright ideas	• challenging pupils to provide explanations and connections, as well as information • sharing and encouraging pupils' curiosity, allowing them to speculate without necessarily needing the correct answer
Pupils as researchers	• enriching and extending their breadth of knowledge by drawing on information that goes beyond that provided for most pupils, including going beyond the National Curriculum • giving pupils access to more demanding texts or ICT-based information for research
Problem solving	• sharing and encouraging pupils' curiosity, allowing them to speculate without necessarily needing the correct answer • applying a higher level of skill to a common question or problem to be solved by the whole class
Investigations	• occasionally giving pupils the chance to modify an investigation to make it more challenging

Infusion has been discussed as a means of incorporating thinking skills explicitly into a curriculum area (see Chapter 1). Hence higher order thinking is in the box at the centre of the model in Figure 2.1, as all this will be encouraged within all the above challenge strategies and within all science lessons. We see this as a key that provides challenge to unlock potential.

Questioning, ICT and creativity stand within the central circle in Figure 2.1 as features that run throughout all the suggested strategies and which can be used to further children's learning. Questioning is a key skill that the teacher brings to all science lessons to optimise the pupils' opportunities to access higher order thinking. ICT is a tool which has the potential to enhance and facilitate science teaching and can be used to increase the level of challenge. We have included creativity in the model to acknowledge the fact that each teacher's imagination and creative thinking will be involved in developing challenging activities for their own particular class. Our model is intended to be a springboard for further ideas, rather than an end in itself. It is hoped that teachers will try some of the challenge strategies and then go on to develop many more of their own.

Outside the circle are organisational strategies that can be used to maximise challenge, such as pupil grouping. The challenge strategies are appropriate for mixed ability classes and all types of groupings. It is possible to use them with the whole class to aid in the identification of able scientists. This method of teaching will have the added bonus of raising the standards, attainment, and motivation of the whole class, not just the most able.

Sometimes an able pupil is deliberately grouped with a less able pupil so that he or she can take on a supportive role. However, while some able pupils are very good at this, it is not necessarily always the case and it very much depends on the individual. It is certainly not appropriate or fair for an able pupil always to be asked to take on this role.

There are occasions when it is helpful to consider grouping the pupils who are able in science together, such as when performing investigations so that they can bounce ideas off each other and enjoy working with others on a similar intellectual level. They will 'benefit academically and socially from spending some time learning alongside other children of similar ability levels to themselves' (Porter 1999).

Similarly there are times when it is worth considering the compacting of the curriculum for some children, that is compressing the content so that they can work through it in a shorter time. The curriculum can be compacted if a gifted child demonstrates mastery of a particular unit of work. This will allow more time to be spent on opportunities to broaden and deepen the curriculum for them. Rogers (1999) highlights the important fact that repetition of work for able pupils might be counter-productive and result in them understanding less and not more at the end of the unit of work. They may tend to switch off and become disengaged if they repeat work that they have already covered and understood. This suggests then that repetitive revision in Year 6 for Key Stage 2 SATs may be, in fact, detrimental rather than helpful. Formative assessment will determine whether the pupil has knowledge and understanding to compact the normal classroom activities.

The second element in the organisational strategy box of Figure 2.1 is appropriate recording. Recording involves the use of any medium to communicate findings and understanding and does not necessitate excessive written work. This is discussed in Chapter 3, 'Assessment'.

Teachers' questions

Kerry and Kerry (2000) consider the centrality of teaching skills in improving able pupil education. They pinpoint effective questioning to be one of the key skill areas for teaching and point out that questions can be formulated to attract mainly lower order thinking or mainly higher order thinking:

> Revision questions and those requiring only the representation of known material (simple comprehension) attract low order answers; while questions that ask students to deduce, hypothesise, analyse, apply, synthesise, evaluate, compare, contrast or imagine attract higher order responses.
>
> (Kerry and Kerry 2000)

Kerry (1981) highlights the fact that the quality of the thought processes should be paramount, not the quantity. As teachers, we tend to use questions for many and varied purposes, such as maintaining pace and keeping the pupils' attention. Hence there tend to be many questions asked in the course of a lesson. Once again, the value of a constant awareness of the encouragement of higher thinking is an invaluable tool for challenge. It is important that the questions are phrased in such a way that they require complex responses, which can then offer progressive and productive challenges to the pupils (Fisher 1995).

It is possible to use Bloom's (1956) taxonomy to categorise questions (see Table 2.2). These categories can be used to frame questions to be used during a science lesson. This enriches the teaching of the lesson as it will enable the teacher to focus on more than recall of information and serve to focus more able children's thinking in a challenging manner.

Table 2.2 Question cues categorised according to higher order thinking skills

Higher order thinking skill	Question cues
Analysis	analyse, separate, order, explain, connect, classify, arrange, divide, compare, select, explain, infer
Synthesis	combine, integrate, modify, rearrange, substitute, plan, create, invent, what if?, compose, prepare, generalise, rewrite
Evaluation	assess, decide, rank, grade, test, measure, recommend, convince, judge, explain, discriminate, support, conclude, compare, summarise

Often pupils will rush to answer a question in a desire to please and to have the teacher's attention, rather than having given the subject any depth of thought. It can therefore be advantageous to allow children to have time to consider questions, and Fisher (1990) suggests that giving children time to think, rather than rushing them to respond, encourages access to the higher order thinking skills. It can be effective to 'drop in' probing questions to a group of children and then come back later to find out how their thoughts and work have progressed. If we, for example, change the question, 'What do you know?' to 'How do you know?' pupils scientific thinking is being challenged and we are beginning to teach them the essence of science.

Another very effective method for improving the quality of pupils' responses by giving them time to think is to use the 'think, pair, share' strategy. This involves posing a question to the class but not taking immediate answers. The pupils are given two minutes to think individually; two minutes to discuss their thoughts with a partner and only then are responses collected.

Challenge strategies

Bright ideas time

Delivering the content of the science curriculum can seem such a big task for teachers and there is often a concern that there is too much content to be covered to allow pupils time to 'indulge' in any deep thinking. However, there are ways of encouraging such thinking while also ensuring that the necessary content is covered.

Professor Philip Adey (1994) has made the important point that:

> What the research shows consistently is that if you face children with intellectual challenges and then help them talk through the problems towards a solution, then you almost literally stretch their minds. They become cleverer, not only in the particular topic, but across the curriculum.

It can therefore be argued that teachers cannot afford to allow their pupils to miss out on the opportunities for deep thinking.

One method of ensuring this is to incorporate a 'bright ideas' slot into lessons and this need not take more than ten minutes per session. Science is surely all about thinking and the enjoyment of thinking deeply. Discussing big ideas is more important than finding the right answer and it will obviously be important to establish a classroom atmosphere in which all ideas and responses will be valued. Asking the pupils to 'think, pair, share' for this slot encourages them to take time to think and will generally improve the depth of their answers. It also increases their participation and involvement.

There are many possible methods for prompting discussion within such a slot, some of these are shown in Table 2.3 and are expanded on the following pages.

Table 2.3 Ideas for prompting discussion during 'bright ideas time'

Prompt	Example
Odd one out	Chocolate, paper and water
PMI (positives, minuses, interesting)	Chocolate door handles
Hot seating	Being Galileo to persuade people that the Earth goes around the Sun
A big question	How do we know that the Earth is a sphere?
Concept cartoons	The snowman's coat

De Bono (1986) and Fisher (1990) are among the many who have considered and developed methods to improve children's thinking. Some of these, such as hot seating and 'PMI' (positives, minuses, interesting) lend themselves particularly well to a bright ideas time in a science lesson. Hot seating involves a child taking the role of, for example a famous scientist, and answering questions from the rest of the class in that role. PMI involves considering the positives, minuses and interesting points related to a specific topic or idea.

Mike Dennis at Curioxity, the hands-on science centre in Oxford, has developed the use of TV game shows, such as *Odd One Out*, to provoke thinking in science. (Dennis 2002).

The concept cartoons of Naylor and Keogh (2000) are very well suited to promoting discussion in a bright ideas time. These cartoons portray a particular situation and cartoon characters state their scientific understanding of what is going on or they postulate what will happen next. Naylor and Keogh have been careful to include many common misconceptions within these statements and so the cartoons are a wonderful source for discussions and sharing of ideas. They can also be used as prompts for investigations to discover what actually will happen or prompts for research to discover more about the scientific ideas behind the situation. They are carefully organised into curriculum areas and have notes about each picture and the science behind it so that the teacher can be confident in enabling the discussion.

It is possible to extend the use of the cartoons by blanking out the speech bubbles and asking the pupils to make up their own comments to put inside them. Also they can try using computer Clip Art to create their own concept cartoons. An example of one of these cartoons is shown later in Figure 2.3, which shows one of Naylor and Keogh's concept cartoons to encourage children to think and discuss what will happen if a coat is put on a snowman. The cartoon can prompt an investigation (see Chapter 6) which models the scenario and can be followed by further discussion in the light of results.

Odd one out: Sc3 Materials and their properties

Chocolate, paper and water

Which is the odd one out?

Three different materials, such as those given above, can be shown to the pupils and they are asked to say which one is the odd one out and why. One advantage of this exercise is that there is not one correct answer.

In the above example, water can be considered to be the odd one out for a number of reasons. For example, it is the only liquid or it is the only one that does not come from a plant. Paper can be the odd one out because it is the only one that is not normally swallowed. Water, in the form of ice, and chocolate will both melt when heated but paper will char and burn. Chocolate can be the odd one out because it is the only one that I like eating at coffee time!

The ensuing discussion will give the pupils the opportunity to be creative in their thinking and they will need to draw on their understanding of the properties of the materials involved.

The discussion can be extended in various ways, such as considering the uses of the materials in relation to their properties. A more challenging extension is to ask them to think about how their brain recognises that water is a liquid and paper is a solid.

PMI: Sc3 Materials and their properties

Chocolate door handles

Pupils are expected to consider the properties of different materials and relate these to their uses. A PMI exercise can be undertaken to consider the positives, minuses and interesting ideas involved in making door handles from chocolate.

Positive: We will never go hungry.
Minus: We will be stuck inside rooms in the summer when the door handles have melted.
Interesting: Rooms can have door handles moulded to suit the season, e.g. eggs at Easter, Santas at Christmas.

Hot seating: Sc4 Physical processes

You are Galileo – persuade people that the Earth goes around the Sun

In 1609 Galileo built a series of telescopes. He described his discoveries in 1610 in his book, Message from the Stars. Galileo claimed:

- He had seen mountains on the Moon.
- The Milky Way is made up of tiny stars.
- There are four small bodies orbiting Jupiter.

In 1613, after moving to Florence, he discovered that Venus shows phases like those of the Moon and therefore must orbit the Sun and not the Earth.

There were two theories around at the time:

- Copernicus' theory that everything goes around the Sun.
- Tycho's theory that everything but the Earth and Moon go around the Sun, which in turn goes around the Earth.

Most astronomers favoured the Tychonic theory but Galileo argued for Copernicus. Eventually Galileo was put on trial in Rome for heresy. He was condemned to house arrest for life (by the standards of his time he got off lightly).

Pupils can be given the facts above and be encouraged to carry out further research on Galileo (a good route for their research is http://www.yahooligans.com).

An alternative way of presenting information is to read the book Starry Messenger (Sis1996), which sets out Galileo's story in a picture book. It is a fascinating and poignant tale.

Having the relevant information, a pupil can then take their place in the hot seat and be questioned by the rest of the class or group about the Copernican model of space. The pupil will need to defend the idea that the Earth moves around the Sun, rather than the Sun moving around the Earth.

A big question: Sc4 Physical processes

How do we know that the Earth is a sphere?

Astronomy is, by definition, an infinite topic, which has huge potential for stretching the mind. The universe is awesome and wonderful. The content of the National Curriculum here is, of necessity, rather limited but its brevity should not hide the immensity of the topics it covers.

The pupils are expected to understand that the Sun, Earth and Moon are approximately spherical. The fact that the Earth (Figure 2.2) is a sphere may seem blatantly obvious to the adult who has grown up with pictures of the Earth taken from space (and the ubiquitous school globe) but the theory was well established before the first space flight. In fact, the ancient Greeks were aware of a spherical Earth and those who first set out to sail around the world were also fairly sure – yet the Earth looks fairly flat to me!

Figure 2.2 The Earth

It is therefore more mind stretching to ask the children to consider how they know that the Earth is a sphere, but not allowing them to include photographs from space in their answers.

This is an interesting discussion starter and it is a surprisingly mind-stretching topic. Some of the evidence is as follows:

- When a ship disappears over the horizon, the last thing to be seen is the mast.
- The Moon and the Sun appear to be circular so perhaps the Earth is too.

Concept cartoon: Sc3 Materials and their properties

Figure 2.3 The snowman's coat – an example of a concept cartoon (Source: Naylor and Keogh 2000)

Pupils as researchers

Porter (1999) highlights the need for gifted learners to be challenged through open-ended activities, which include the opportunities for children to pursue their own interests to a depth that satisfies them. Allowing the children to act as researchers provides obvious potential for this to be the case. However, it is not acceptable to just ask the pupils to find out more about a particular topic. This research needs careful direction from the teacher so that it is really challenging and motivating. This can be achieved in imaginative and interesting ways so that it goes beyond a simple request to find out more about a particular subject.

Research gives pupils opportunities to venture into areas of science not normally covered in primary school. One of the inevitable, potential drawbacks of primary science is that the children can miss out on the excitement of some of the fascinating big concepts in science. These are the theories that underpin the basic facts, such as the existence of atoms and electrons, or at the other end of the scale, galaxies and black holes etc. Able children can thoroughly enjoy this type of challenge and asking them to undertake structured research can give them the opportunity to explore more complex systems and ideas. Hence the big concepts form a possible extension activity as they go beyond the primary curriculum. There is a range of websites and books suitable for school libraries that introduce these ideas in a fun way. A selection of websites are referred to throughout the subsequent chapters and there are numerous books which can be used to encourage exciting research, such as *What's the Big Idea?* series (1997–9) from Hodder Children's Books, the children's division of Hodder and Stoughton.

A search engine which is especially designed for use by children is http://www.yahooligans.com. Adult search engines such as http://www.google.com contain advanced search tools into which all the words or the exact phrase can be inserted so that the search is highly specific.

Example: Sc2 Life processes and living things

Using the CD-ROM *The Ultimate Human Body* (Dorling Kindersley 1994) the pupils can investigate how the heart and circulatory systems work and link this to their investigations about pulse rate. They can then feed back this information to the rest of the class. They will be using evaluation skills to firstly set out criteria for the information they are wanting to present and then judging what information is relevant and why.

Problem solving

Problem solving is a very effective way of challenging able children. As Clark and Callow (1998) point out, pupils' interest is often gained by posing a question that is intriguing, and sustained by the motivation to puzzle something out.

However, it is not always completely clear what is actually meant by the phrase, 'problem solving'. Montgomery (1996) notes that it will involve a situation in which there is no one correct answer or solution and hence it will be 'fuzzy'. Fisher (1990) points out that, in contrast, schoolchildren are most commonly presented with 'closed problems', the type that focus on the search for one right answer. He contends that the ability of a child to apply his or her thinking to the solving of open problems will be a key to success in life.

Problem solving involves the setting of activities, which require the pupils to draw on their scientific knowledge and skills, to apply them and explore more complex ideas. Montgomery (1996) notes that a characteristic of a problem-solving approach is that there needs to be plenty of content material. She also makes the interesting contention that, in the process of searching this content for clues and ideas to solve the problem, much is committed to memory incidentally. As is often the case, involvement in a task has many beneficial by-products.

Problem solving is part of our lives and things are rarely closed and straightforward so it is therefore an essential skill for every future citizen, which can only be learned first-hand. With problem solving, the focus is on knowledge, skills and concept acquisition through enquiry-based learning (Eyre 1997).

Problem solving involves defining problems, thinking up different solutions and then testing them. Problem solving therefore, draws on components of both critical and creative thinking. Although problems may be different and diverse they are best tackled using a range of process skills. These skills include:

- identifying and understanding a problem
- discussing, researching and proposing solutions to the problem
- planning and carrying out an investigation to solve the problem, or designing and building a device to meet the criteria set in the problem
- monitoring progress in tackling the problem
- testing, evaluating and modifying the device or solutions to the problems.

The problems are best related to real-life situations, such as designing an alarm system, as described in Chapter 7. Problem solving can begin simply with a sequence of activities where children are getting first-hand experience by 'playing' with science resources. This will allow children time to make free observations and work out ideas, which might then be developed into a solution to a problem. Pupils might combine science and design and technology ideas to produce a lighthouse with a flashing light after exploring (playing with) simple circuits and switches. There is obviously a clear link in such a manner between science and design and technology.

Pupils who are seen to be highly able in design and technology tend to have 'creative ideas and can develop them successfully . . . persevering with the problems encountered' (Dudley LEA 1998). Other more specific characteristics related to design and technology have been defined by Lewin (1999) and include 'seeing the same as everyone else and thinking something different, high spatial sense and practical and mechanical ability.' These types of characteristics may be indicators for future high calibre engineers.

The National Curriculum for 2000 sets out clear aims for primary children. It should 'enable pupils to think creatively and critically and to solve problems' (DfEE/QCA 1999). Within this curriculum design and technology is defined as preparing:

> pupils to participate in tomorrow's rapidly changing technologies . . . The subject calls for pupils to become autonomous and creative problem solvers, as individuals and members of a team . . . They combine practical skills with an understanding of aesthetics, social and environmental issues, function and industrial practice.
>
> (DfEE/QCA 1999)

In terms of the relationship between science and design and technology, the scientific knowledge which pupils use to test and develop their ideas, can be used in technology to help solve problems. Children might use their knowledge of forces and friction to produce a streamlined train or of electricity to produce a circuit to wire a model house. Montague-Smith and Winstone (1998) have summarised this relationship between science and design and technology as shown in Table 2.4.

Enriching the curriculum using a social interactional approach introduces tasks that require teamwork and the possibility for different views to emerge. It encourages flexible thinking and creativity within the group. For reasons addressed earlier, it is beneficial sometimes to allow the able pupils to work together in a problem-solving context.

Table 2.4 The relationship between science and design and technology (*Source:* Montague-Smith and Winstone 1998)

Science	**Design and technology**
Using the specifically scientific skills of investigating and experimenting to test ideas	Using the specifically design and technology skills of devising ways to solve problems
Generating and testing scientific ideas	Designing and making a product, using the skills of making and knowledge about materials
Reflecting critically on the way evidence has been gathered and used in testing ideas	Evaluating the finished product, looking at ways in which it could be improved

Example: Sc4 Physical processes

> **Hamster in danger!**
>
> **Wire up the cage so that an alarm is raised if anyone opens the door.**
>
> To save the hamster from too much stress, the pupils can be encouraged to make a mock cage from a shoe box for the testing of their designs.

Example: Sc3 Materials and their properties

> **The head teacher's sugar has been spilt in the sandpit and she wants it back for her cup of coffee!**
>
> This scenario can be introduced to pupils before or after having met the concept of dissolving. It will be more stretching if used as an introduction to dissolving. It can also be used as a lively revision tool when the pupils have not revised this area for a while.

Science resources

The following is a list of resources that we feel are invaluable for developing a challenging primary science curriculum:

- Goldsworthy, A. and Feasey, R. (1997) *Making Sense of Primary Science Investigations*. Hatfield: Association for Science Education.
  A very useful text for considering Sc1, an area of huge potential for able children.
- Goldsworthy, A., Watson, J. R. and Wood-Robinson, V. (1999) *Investigations: Getting to grips with graphs*. Hatfield: Association for Science Education.
- Goldsworthy, A., Watson, J. R. and Wood-Robinson, V. (2000) *Investigations: Developing understanding*. Hatfield: Association for Science Education.
  Both the above packages are designed for the Key Stage 2/3 transition groups.
- Naylor, S. and Keogh, B. (2000) *Concept Cartoons in Science Education*. Sandbach: Millgate House Publishers. A brilliant method of provoking discussion and encouraging children to think about science. It can be extended in many ways, such as asking children to design their own concept cartoons.

In addition to these resources, the Ginn *New STAR Science* series is an excellent scheme, which has well-designed questions for challenge and is linked to the QCA Scheme of Work:

- Feasey, R., Goldsworthy, A., Phipps, R. and Stringer, J. (2001) *New STAR Science Series*. Oxford: Ginn.

If the purchase of the whole scheme is beyond the school's budget, the photocopiable resources related to Sc1 can be purchased separately:

- Feasey, R., Goldsworthy, A., Phipps, R. and Stringer, J. (2001) *New STAR Science. Teaching scientific enquiry lower junior.* Oxford: Ginn.
- Feasey, R., Goldsworthy, A., Phipps, R. and Stringer, J. (2001) *New STAR Science. Teaching scientific enquiry upper junior.* Oxford: Ginn.

3 Assessment

Assessment is rightly considered to be a vital element in the teaching and learning process but it may be helpful to stand back and consider some fundamental questions, particularly in relation to able pupils:

- Why do we assess?
- What do we assess?
- How do we assess?

Each of these will be considered in turn.

Why do we assess?

Teachers make assessments in order to gather information, which is relevant to learning objectives, the content of the curriculum, how well children have achieved the objectives, and the strategies used to meet the objectives. Teachers are constantly evaluating both their own teaching and the children's performance. For assessment to be meaningful, it needs to sit alongside and feed into future planning. This point is clearly emphasised by the Assessment Reform Group (1999) who stated that teachers should decide how and when they would assess children's learning at the same time as they plan the work. The results of that ongoing assessment will then feed into future work.

There obviously needs to be a good match between the pupils' ability, the work set and the assessment process (QCA 2001a). Assessment is important because it determines the appropriate level of work planned for able children, so that they are given every opportunity to develop to their full potential. Able pupils can sometimes surprise us with their depth of understanding and thinking. A group of Year 6 children were asked how they know that the Earth is a sphere. They were not allowed to use pictures from space as an answer because the ancient Greeks were fairly confident that the Earth was a sphere, long before space travel was established. The response from one of the pupils was: 'Because gravity comes from the centre of the earth, because a sphere is the smallest shape you can make from the centre, it would most likely be pulled up into a sphere.' In this amazing response, he has taken and applied his understanding of gravity pulling towards the centre of the Earth. He has then worked out the fact that, as it pulls in towards the centre, it will pull equally in all directions and so the likely shape to result is a sphere. The teacher asking the question expected an answer that gave evidence for the Earth being a sphere, such as a ship coming over the horizon is seen mast first and then the rest comes into view. Instead, the response was theoretical, worked from first principles and completely correct.

To teach a child of this ability can seem a daunting prospect and appropriate provision will need to be high in cognitive challenge so that she or he remains engaged. The strategies that have been presented in this book should go some way to providing the enriched learning environment in which such a mind should flourish.

For assessment to be effective it needs to be both ongoing (formative) and at the end of units of work (summative). Too often it seems that summative assessment is seen to be all important and drives the teaching process, as will be discussed later.

Both formative and summative assessments are necessary, but it is formative assessment that has particular potential to take children's learning forward:

> Day-to-day (formative) assessment is a powerful mechanism for providing feedback to pupils and helping them to reflect on their learning. All pupils benefit from gaining insight into the way in which they learn, and gifted and talented pupils will normally be quick to apply these insights to further learning, increasing their autonomy and independence.
>
> (QCA 2001a)

Formative assessment is an active, rather than a passive, process which can play a vital role in encouraging pupils to advance their learning and in giving them the necessary information to facilitate this.

However, the information provided by summative assessment is essential for a range of interested parties, such as parents and colleagues. As pupils go on to new classes to be with different teachers, the transfer of assessment information is crucial for the continuity of appropriate provision. This is even more the case at major transition points that involve a change in schools. Ofsted (2002) noted that overall there were wide variations in schools' expectations of pupils' progress during Key Stage 3. In the case of the boy quoted above when he progresses to Key Stage 3, it will become the secondary school's responsibility to encourage and nurture his thinking and the progression in his learning. In order to do this effectively, they will need to have received and used information about his ability, achievements and potential.

What do we assess?

We have discussed the infusion approach to the teaching of thinking skills through the science curriculum and the advantages of including learning objectives that overtly encourage the pupils' use of higher order thinking. It is obviously important to assess these learning objectives, so we need to consider how the pupils' use of higher order thinking can be assessed. Requiring the pupils simply to record what they did in the lesson obviously will not achieve this end.

Black and Wiliam (1998) note that, for primary teachers particularly, there is a tendency to emphasise quantity and presentation of work rather than its quality in relation to learning. It is important, among other things, to consider carefully the need to encourage the pupils to record their work in a relevant and appropriate way. The challenge for teachers is to find realistic means of assessing the pupils' progress and to give feedback in a way that helps them to further their own learning.

How do we assess?

We have said that assessment is an active process, which involves giving feedback to the pupils and this can take place in a variety of ways. It also has a variety of benefits, which can be summed up as follows:

> Feedback on how work can be improved and clear learning and assessment objectives provide gifted and talented pupils with an agenda for progress and enables teachers to plan future work to meet individual needs more closely and set appropriate targets. Positive and constructive feedback also has a major part to play in affirming a pupil's self-esteem and increasing motivation.
>
> (QCA 2001a)

This highlights the stages in assessment: the setting and communicating of the learning objectives; the feedback to the pupils; the consequent adaptation of the teacher's planning and the effect on pupils' self-esteem and learning. Each of these will be considered in turn.

Learning objectives

Goldsworthy *et al.* (2000b) have developed a model for using classroom assessment for learning, which they have called targeted learning. While this is specifically related to scientific enquiry, the principles behind it have a wider application. They highlight the need to share clearly with the pupils the aims of the lesson and that this can be done in a variety of ways:

- by telling the whole class
- in discussion with groups or individuals
- by writing the aims in a public place.

They found that, in general, the communication of aims was more successful when a combination of these methods was used. Within scientific enquiry, it is particularly important to direct the pupils' attention to the fact that it is often a process of the investigation that is the focus for the learning. For example, if the pupils are asked to make a prediction related to the question, 'Can the people with the strongest legs jump the furthest?' they may think that the focus is finding out about legs, rather than the skill of making a scientific prediction.

Feedback

Feedback is provided by dialogue between the teacher and pupil, either verbally or in written form. Goldsworthy *et al.* (2000b) highlight the need for pupils not just to know that they have done well or badly, but to understand just what they have done well or badly. The assessment also needs to take into account the expectations for that particular pupil. Hence the more able will be expected to demonstrate their ability to use higher order thinking.

Providing oral feedback during lessons is a key skill which involves teachers thinking on their feet and often introducing prompt questions to further the pupils' progress and to encourage a greater depth of thinking. Teacher questioning has been considered in more detail in Chapter 2, 'Planning for Challenge'. If the teacher has a notebook, any significant comments made by individual pupils can be recorded as evidence of their developing thinking and understanding.

Qualitative written feedback on work is usually of more value than the giving of a quantitative mark. It is evidently more time consuming to give a written comment but it has the advantage of communicating to the pupil the fact that their work has been given serious consideration and has therefore been valued. It can also direct the pupil to an understanding of how they can take their learning forward.

As Eyre (1997) notes, able children are capable of assessing and evaluating their own work and they should be encouraged to develop these skills. Hence the pupils need to be actively involved in the assessment process and encouraged in the skill of self-reflection. It is therefore important to ensure that sufficient time is allowed for them to evaluate their work. Evaluation is a recognised component of an investigation but in many respects, it should be a core feature of all work undertaken.

The timing of more formal assessments is important and it is interesting to reflect on the fact that it is common for them to take place at the end of units of work. However, such information may be of more use during the unit so that the pupils can receive feedback on their understanding while time remains for them to do something about it.

Adaptation of planning

Figure 3.1 is a model for assessment that summarises the points raised in this chapter and previous discussions about identification of ability in science. In this it can be seen that, by an infusion approach, an enriched learning environment is provided for all the class. The pupils of particular scientific

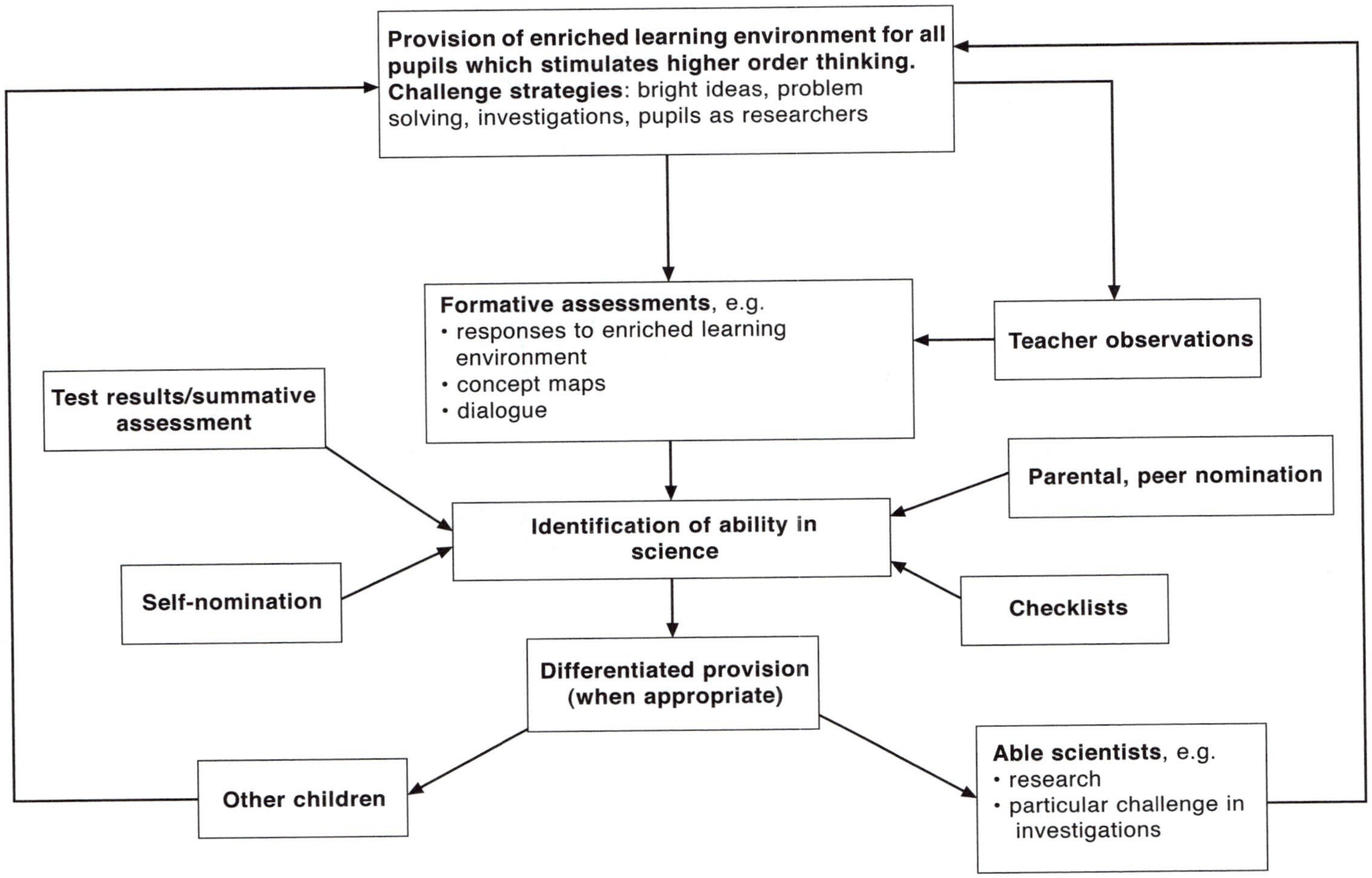

Figure 3.1 A model for assessment

ability will be identified through a combination of summative and formative assessments, possibly linking to information from parents, peers and the pupils themselves. Checklists may also be helpful in this process. This then feeds into the planning of differentiation so that individuals' needs can be met. Strategies can be put into place to ensure an appropriate level of challenge and expectation for the able scientists, such as the encouragement of independence through directed pupil research and ability grouping in some investigations.

Self-esteem and learning

Eyre's model (1997) has already been discussed in Chapter 1:

Ability + Opportunity/Support + Motivation = Achievement

As pupils are given opportunities to develop and demonstrate their thinking and receive subsequent feedback, it is likely that their motivation will be increased. This may be the case for the pupils who are able in science but not necessarily in other subjects. For example, we interviewed one teacher who was involved in the AstraZeneca project, 'Conceptual Challenge in Primary Science for Year 6 Pupils'. She encouraged the children to respond verbally during Bright ideas sessions and through this identified two boys as being able in science. This ability was not at all evident in other subjects and their behaviour was often a problem. Their self-esteem was raised through achievement in science, which then had a positive effect on their attitude and behaviour.

However, Black and Wiliam (1998) point out the fact that an emphasis on the challenge to think for yourself (and not just work harder) can be disturbing to many. We have had experience of able children who are used to achieving highly and 'getting everything right' but who became unhappy and disorientated when their prediction in relation to the outcome of an investigation proved to be incorrect. This is an important experience for able children as they can then learn to reflect on their work and adjust their understanding and thinking accordingly, within a supportive environment.

Practical ways of assessing within each of the suggested challenge strategies in this book will be discussed in turn.

Bright ideas

The bright ideas time will tend to be discussion based and so it can be difficult to keep a record of pupils' comments. However, this will hopefully be an ideal opportunity for the pupils to reveal their depth of thinking. One method of capturing this is occasionally to give the pupils the discussion question or prompt activity on a piece of paper so that they can record their thoughts, by either writing or drawing. Another method is to make use of a classroom assistant and to ask them to note the pupils' verbal responses. If the 'think, pair, share' strategy is used, the pupils can be asked to feedback from their pair on a Post-it note which is then placed on a wall or board. The Post-its then provide a record of their thoughts.

Pupils as researchers

Having undertaken a piece of research, the findings can be fed back to the rest of the class in a variety of ways. This can take the form of, for example, a verbal report, a PowerPoint presentation, a hot-seating session or a newspaper report. It will be possible to analyse the result in terms of the thinking involved. For example, when pairs of Year 6 children were asked to produce a foreign correspondent's report from a planet, there was an obvious variation in the quality of the final product. One pair merely read information that they had downloaded from the Internet, while another pair took the information and used it to produce an imaginative and exciting three-minute talk. The teacher took brief notes during the talks to produce a record of her assessment. The pupils were also asked to reflect on and evaluate their own presentations.

Problem solving

If the problem solving has been practically based, then the final product forms a record of achievement. A digital photo may be all that is needed for a permanent record. It is often possible for the teacher to rate the level of sophistication of the solution to the given problem.

For example, a group of children was asked to use their electrical skills to develop a system to display a jewel safely. The most sophisticated solutions, involved the construction of an automatic switch that activated an alarm when the jewel was touched or moved, or the door to the room was opened. A slightly less sophisticated version involved the construction of an alarm that was activated when the door of the room was closed, rather than opened. Generally, it is more useful to have an alarm sound when a door has been opened, although one group justified this by explaining that the burglar would shut the door after him so that he could not be seen! Finally, some solutions involved the use of a switch that was not automatic and had to be activated by a 'pretend' guard in the vicinity. The teacher made brief notes on the level of sophistication as each group demonstrated their solution to the rest of the class.

Investigations

Investigations are discussed in Chapter 4 and it is suggested that it is often beneficial to focus the learning objectives on particular strands within Sc1, such as the making of a scientific prediction. The assessment then obviously needs to be related to this and it is usually possible to assess or rate the level of sophistication of the work, in a similar way to that suggested for problem solving.

We will once again consider the investigation, 'Can the people with the strongest legs jump the furthest?' A group of children were asked to record their predictions and below is a sample of their unedited replies. These were able lower primary pupils and initially their arguments tended to be circular, 'The people with the strongest legs jump the furthest because they have the strongest legs.' They were asked why they felt this to be the case and they needed a degree of encouragement to take their reasoning further:

1. There is no reason.
2. Most of the time people jump further when they are stronger.
3. The people with the stronger legs are strong so they can jump higher.
4. Muscles has got nothing to do with how far because muscles are if you carry heavy things not how far you go.
5. I think the people with the lightest legs will jump the highest because they don't have to lift as much.
6. I think the strongest legs will push the most and go the furthest.

It is possible quite quickly to rate these responses, according to the depth of thinking involved. The first response demonstrates the fact that this pupil was not able, at this time, to take the argument beyond the original circular one and this was true of a number of the class. Pupils 2 and 3 introduced the word, 'strong', but again the argument tended to remain circular. Pupil 4 was beginning to think around the problem and was wondering about the function of a person's muscles. Pupils 5 and 6 were demonstrating considerable depth in their thinking. Pupil 5 has, with good reason, re-evaluated his original prediction and pupil 6 has drawn on her existing scientific understanding of forces.

Any of the strands within Sc1 provide opportunities for this type of assessment. Processes such as the interpretations of results, looking for patterns in data, predicting the shape of a graph etc. all require the use of higher order thinking, as will be discussed in Chapter 4. This type of assessment has the advantage that it requires a minimal amount of recording on the children's part and it is relatively quick for the teacher to rate the response in terms of the use of higher order thinking.

Summative assessment

The level descriptions within each of the attainment targets set out the basis for making judgements about pupils' performance at the end of Key Stages 1, 2 and 3. Able pupils will obviously be expected to gain the higher levels. It is interesting to note that able pupils within Key Stage 2 can demonstrate evidence for being at Level 6 within Sc1, Scientific enquiry, without needing to dip into the content of the Key Stage 3 curriculum. This is not the case for the other areas of the science curriculum, Sc2 to Sc4, as the Level 6 descriptions highlight their need to use knowledge and understanding from the Key Stage 3 content. It is therefore quite justifiable to assess some able Key Stage 2 pupils as being at, or working towards, Level 6 within AT1.

The level descriptions within the National Curriculum are, by necessity, brief and further guidance for expectations of able pupils is given at the end of each unit within the QCA Scheme of Work for science. These expectations are a mixture of both knowledge and understanding linked to higher order thinking, associated with Sc2 to Sc4 and the scientific process, associated with Sc1. The examples provided in Table 3.1 illustrate this.

Table 3.1 Examples of expectations for more able pupils

Unit of work	Expectations for the more able
3B Helping plants grow well	Children will be able to explain why healthy stems are needed for plants to grow; recognise that the leaves of a plant are associated with healthy growth; explain in simple terms why a number of plants should be used to provide reliable evidence about plant growth.
4E Friction	Children will be able to identify friction as a force; describe some ways in which friction between solid surfaces can be increased and identify some trends or patterns in observations and measurements.
6C More about dissolving	Children will be able to present results in a line graph where appropriate; explain why it is important to repeat measurements and how to deal with repeated results when drawing a graph.

An assessment-driven curriculum

There is, however, an inherent danger within the process of summative assessment. As a result of our contacts and research with schools, we have become convinced that in Year 6, in particular, pupils tend to spend a considerable percentage of their science lessons revising and revisiting the facts that are considered necessary to gain the expected grades in the Standard Assessment Tests (SATs). Harrison (2001) points out that an increasing number of teachers are teaching their Year 6 pupils to the science test and that they are teaching tips, tricks and techniques simply to achieve higher percentages. In addition, Black and Wiliam (1998) comment that 'Such tests can dominate teachers' work, and insofar as they encourage drilling to produce right answers to short out-of-context questions, this dominance can draw teachers away from the paths to effective formative work.' Black and Wiliam go on to say that teachers can thereby be constrained to act against their own better judgement about the best way to develop the learning of their pupils. Indeed, teachers can feel that their creativity is being stifled rather than being released for the pupils' benefit. One of the points highlighted by Rogers (1999), in her synthesis of research findings regarding provision for the gifted and talented, is that gifted students are significantly more likely to forget or mislearn science content when they must drill and review it more than two or three times. Hence it can be argued that this type of curriculum can particularly hinder the more able pupils.

This revision can be an arid process, which results in disaffection and Montgomery (2001a) comments that 'What we do know is that boredom and lack of cognitive challenge in the daily curriculum is playing a more significant role in causing pupils across the ability range to become disaffected than was originally suspected.'

From 2003, two significant changes will be made to the Key Stage 2 science SAT papers and it is to be hoped that these will go some way to changing this emphasis on rote revision:

- an increase in the number of questions assessing scientific enquiry
- an increase in the length of time for the papers from 35 minutes to 45 minutes.

The number of questions will not be increased and the intention is to give the children 'sufficient time to think around the issues of scientific enquiry'. Again this lends credence to our contention that children need to be encouraged to think, rather than be subject to rote revision.

Questions in the tests may ask children to:

- describe how an investigation could be carried out
- what factors need to be controlled
- what factors need to be measured
- whether the outcome can be predicted
- how the results are going to be presented
- what the results show and whether they match the prediction
- to explain the outcome whether the evidence collected is significant, reliable and valid.

(QCA 2003)

This should lead to the development of far more open-ended and thought-provoking questions. All of the above require the pupils to use higher order thinking and so we would argue that the best revision for this is to give the pupils the type of enriched learning environment described in this book. As Montgomery (2001b) points out, 'When students at all levels have opportunities to construct their own meaning then they engage in "deep learning" which is secure and does not require revision because it cannot be forgotten.'

Appropriate recording

We have discussed the importance of assessing the quality of pupils' work, rather than quantity or presentation. The way that pupils are required to record their work in science merits consideration in this context.

Practical work and the associated skills should be a key feature of all science lessons. We would go so far as to say that if pupils are spending anywhere near half the lesson writing, then something is radically wrong. The fact that some pupils will be able in science but not necessarily in literacy has already been mentioned and it is unfair to constrain their enjoyment of science by requiring them to write in excessive detail. When asked about his experience of school science, one able Year 4 pupil said: 'We always write down what we think will happen, what we are going to do and then what actually happened, and it is boring!'

In a similar way to assessment, it may be helpful to consider why the pupils need to keep a record of their science work. There can be a number of valid reasons to require them to keep a permanent record, and these include:

- to assess their progress and thinking
- to provide the pupils with formative feedback to take their learning forward
- to provide evidence of the coverage of the curriculum
- to develop skills associated with communication of findings.

Assessment and formative feedback have already been considered so we will take each of the remaining reasons in turn.

Evidence of coverage of the curriculum

Some teachers argue that Ofsted inspectors will trawl the pupils' books for evidence of their science work and so everything needs to be recorded in great detail. However, it is most likely that an imaginative and thoughtful approach will have a more favourable impact than rote recording. The 'methods, results, conclusion' approach does not have a place in primary schools. The pupils' recording of their work needs to be appropriate and relevant. For example, it may be relevant to take a digital photograph of an electrical circuit, or for the pupils to make a poster of their research findings, or record in detail only the part of a scientific investigation that was highlighted for challenge in the learning objectives.

During the AstraZeneca project, 'Conceptual Challenge in Primary Science for Year 6 Pupils', an attitude questionnaire revealed the fact that one class of Year 6 children did not like planning. However, when this class was allowed to plan and carry out an investigation without any detailed written recording of their work, they became avidly engaged in the process. At the end of the session, they were thrilled and commented that it had been a 'really cool' science time. Their planning had been purely verbal but it was both effective and appropriate. In fact, it was the recording in detail of the planning that the pupils did not enjoy, rather than the actual process of planning. Similarly their teacher was thrilled at the level of scientific understanding revealed in the verbal discussion that accompanied their work. It is not a crime sometimes for sessions to take place with no written record from the pupils – the evidence will be in the teacher's planning and, ideally, a short evaluation of the lesson.

The development of skills associated with communication of findings

It is necessary for pupils to learn to communicate their findings and thinking effectively. Creativity can be brought into science by encouraging this communication to take place in imaginative ways, such as on posters or newssheets. A verbal communication can be recorded by audiotaping or videoing. In science it is advantageous to be both clear and succinct and so there is little to be gained from requiring the pupils always to record at great length and certainly nothing to be gained from them copying reams from the blackboard.

4 Sc1 Scientific enquiry

Science should be thought of as a mode of enquiry and not simply a body of knowledge to be learnt. In other words, it is about doing and not just knowing, as the famous scientist once said:

'Why,' said the Dodo, 'the best way to explain it is to do it.'
(Lewis Carroll, *Alice's Adventures in Wonderland*)

Scientific enquiry (Sc1) is taught through contexts taken from the other areas of the National Curriculum, Sc2 Life processes and living things, Sc3 Materials and their properties and Sc4 Physical processes (QCA/DfEE 1999). Sc1 is divided into two strands – ideas and evidence in science and investigative skills. Investigative skills are further divided into:

- Planning;
- Obtaining and presenting evidence; and
- Considering evidence and evaluating.

Figure 4.1 is a diagrammatic representation which shows how Sc1 links with the rest of the science National Curriculum. In this and subsequent similar diagrams, everything above the dark horizontal line denotes factors in the teacher's planning and everything below relates to the activities of the pupils. Hence the teacher plans, using the National Curriculum (which may be subsumed into the QCA Science Scheme of Work), in such a way that the pupils are enabled to plan and perform a scientific investigation.

In order to perform investigations, various scientific processes are necessary. These processes can be considered to be a hierarchy. The simpler process skills include such things as measuring, observing and classifying and we shall call these **core skills**. The more demanding process skills include interpreting data, controlling variables, making predictions etc. and we shall call these **higher order skills**. Figure 4.2 illustrates the fact that the higher order skills build upon the core skills. Therefore, for able children, focusing on the higher order skills will encourage their use of higher order thinking. It is to be noted that this is part of the normal curriculum and it is an area that needs very little 'tinkering' to provide challenge. Both core and higher order skills need to be mastered and this can only be achieved by the pupils being involved in

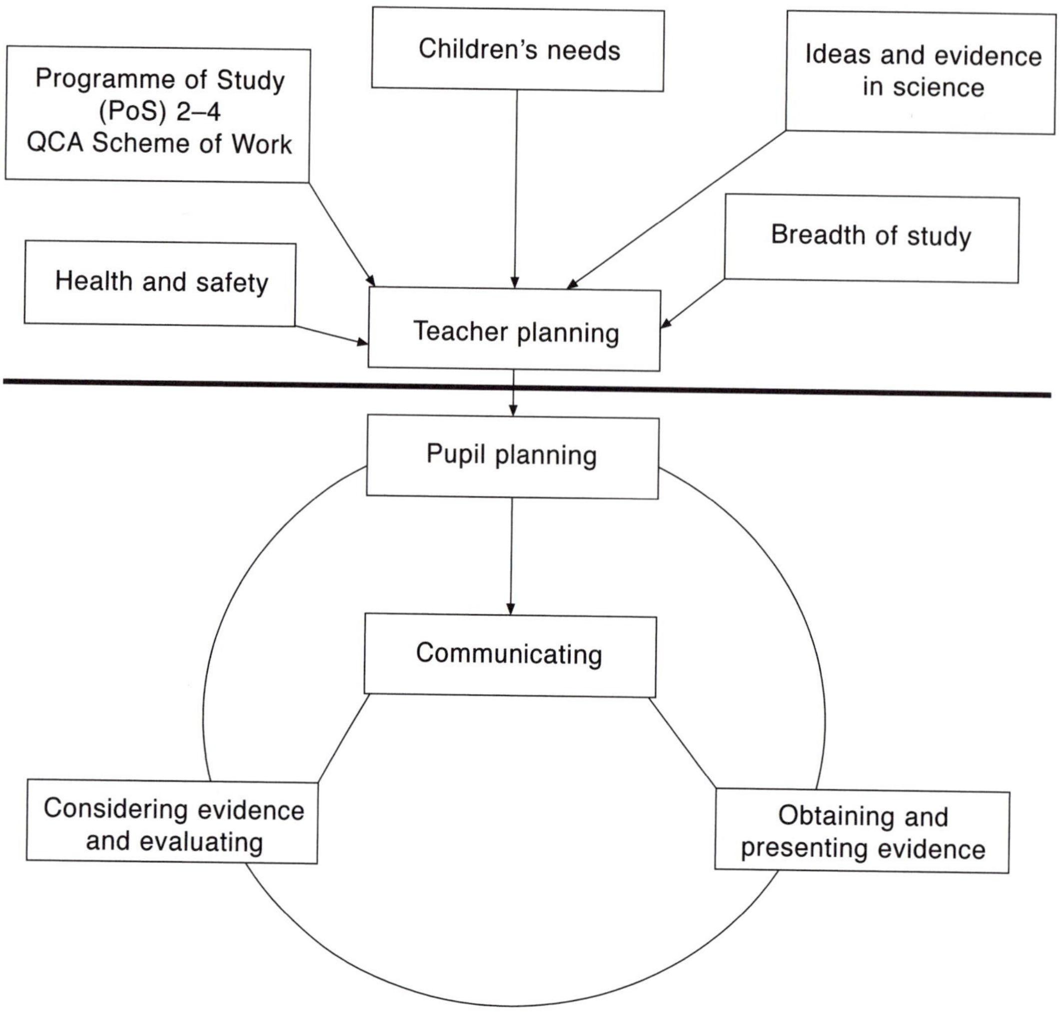

Figure 4.1 Links between Sc1 Scientific enquiry and the rest of the science National Curriculum

practical scientific work or manipulating scientific data. Practical work should be the norm in science lessons – it is one of the elements that makes science different and exciting for the children. Obviously, practical work seems harder to organise in some areas of the curriculum, such as the Earth and beyond. However, the scientific processes are still evident. For example, an observation (core skill) is that we experience night and day and postulating as to why this is so involves higher order thinking.

This whole process of scientific enquiry is the ultimate aim but the skills within it, both core and higher order, need teaching and practising with a purpose. As Goldsworthy and Feasey (1997) point out, investigating is just one type of practical activity in science, albeit a very important one. Practical activities can be grouped into four broad types: basic skills; observations; illustrative work and investigative work. These all have a valid place in primary science lessons and it is important to be clear that not all practical work in science

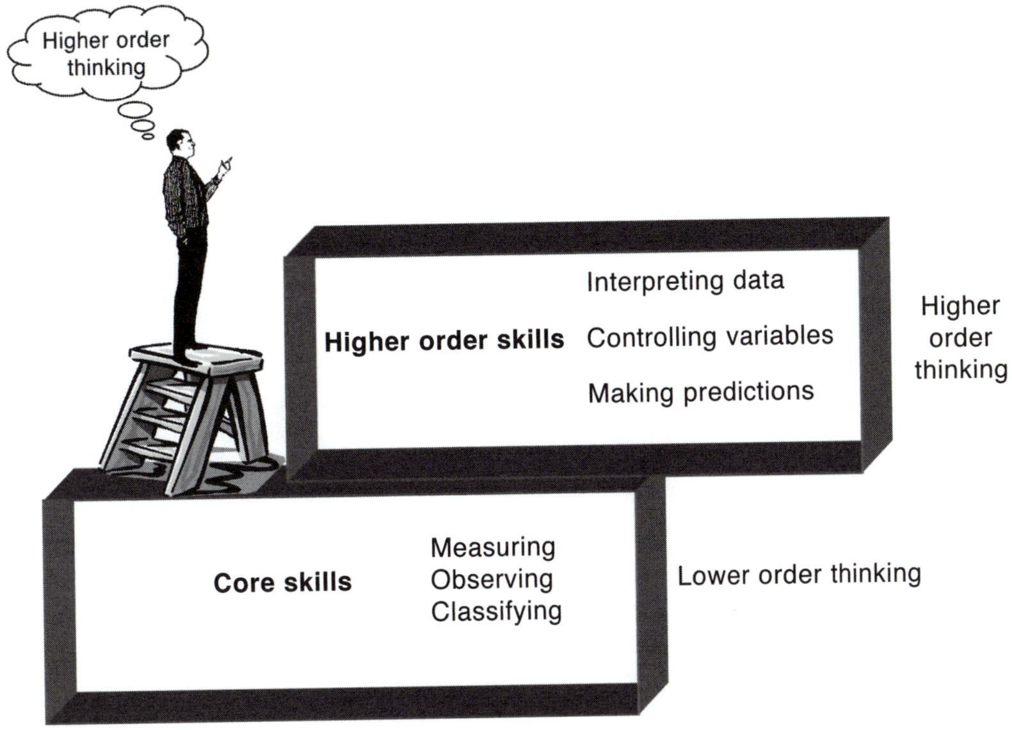

Figure 4.2 Higher order skills build on core skills

can be categorised as investigative. Each of these four types of practical will be considered in turn.

Basic skills

Figure 4.3 is an illustration of this type of practical.

Children obviously need to learn to use the basic equipment necessary for scientific practical work. They also need to learn how to communicate their findings effectively by making tables, plotting graphs etc. Planning activities to enable children to learn and apply these competences is important. Focused questioning from the teacher is vital as it raises children's awareness, understanding of when, and what to measure, what equipment to use and what units of measurement are appropriate. This type of practical work does not generally involve the pupils in the planning and so there is no pupil box for this in Figure 4.3. The work need not be dull and it can be planned in such a way that higher order thinking can be encouraged within it.

For example, children need to be able to use a thermometer. They can be encouraged to hold one in the palm of their hand and observe what happens. They can be asked why they think that the coloured liquid rises and what use can be made of this. They can then measure temperatures of different substances, such as the water in the pond, tap water, water that has been in the kettle for the staff coffee break (now lukewarm).

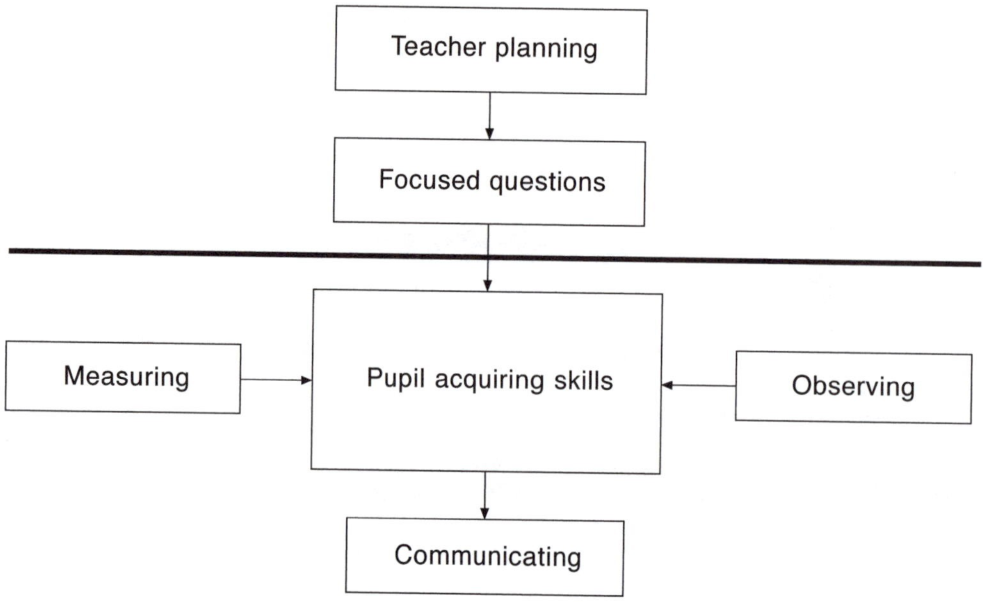

Figure 4.3 Basic skills

In their helpful book, *Teach It! Do It! Let's get to it!* Goldsworthy and Holmes (1999) have drawn out lesson plans for different year groups to illustrate the progression from the acquisition of a necessary competence to its subsequent use in an investigation.

Investigations: 'Getting to grips with 'Graphs' is an invaluable publication developed by Goldsworthy *et al.* (1999) which contains software and photocopiable resources. It is designed to encourage the development of the skills necessary for drawing and interpreting graphs. This is aimed at Key Stages 2 and 3 and so is particularly appropriate for able children in the primary school. As this includes material available for use on a computer, pupils can work through the activities at their own pace. The material progresses beyond the basic competences involved in drawing graphs to their interpretation, the description of patterns and other activities that very much require the use of higher order thinking.

Observations

Figure 4.4 illustrates a practical based on carrying out observations. Observations form the basis of all science. If children are not taught to observe in a wide variety of situations, they will not be equipped to perform investigations. Observation is not a simple skill, it involves all the senses, leading to the ability to compare and contrast, group, classify and recognise patterns. Observations may also trigger questions in children's minds that can lead onto investigations. Teacher's questions should focus the children on what observations to make, how relevant and detailed they should be, and how they relate one with the other. These related observations will allow children to explain phenomena. They are often concerned with natural events where there is no attempt to change things nor make comparisons.

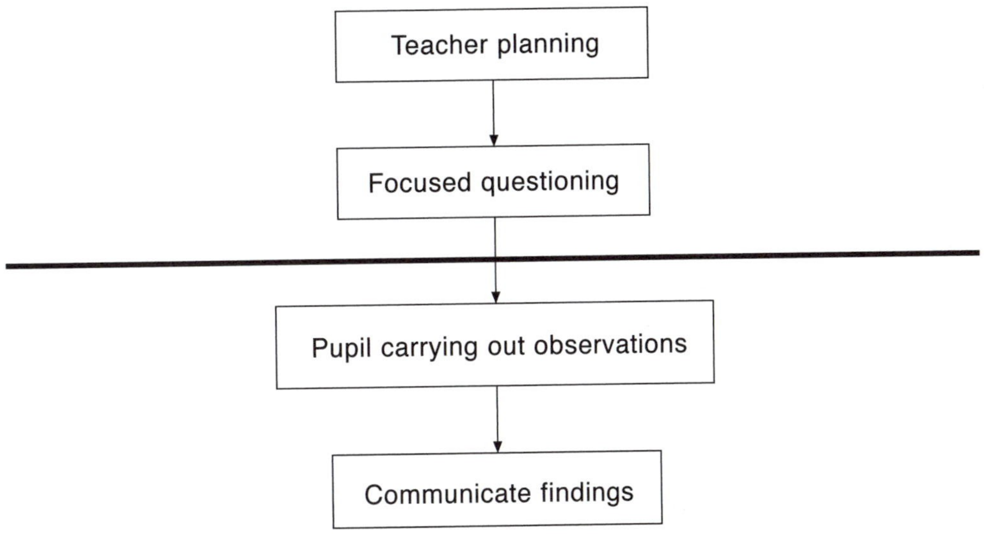

Figure 4.4 Observations

An example of an observations practical is the identification of plants in a hedgerow or species of animals in a pond. This can be extended in such a way that pupils need to draw on their higher order thinking skills. For example, why do these plants or animals tend to be found in these particular locations? How do you think they are adapted to their environment?

Illustrative work

Figure 4.5 shows a teacher-planned and teacher-led activity which determines

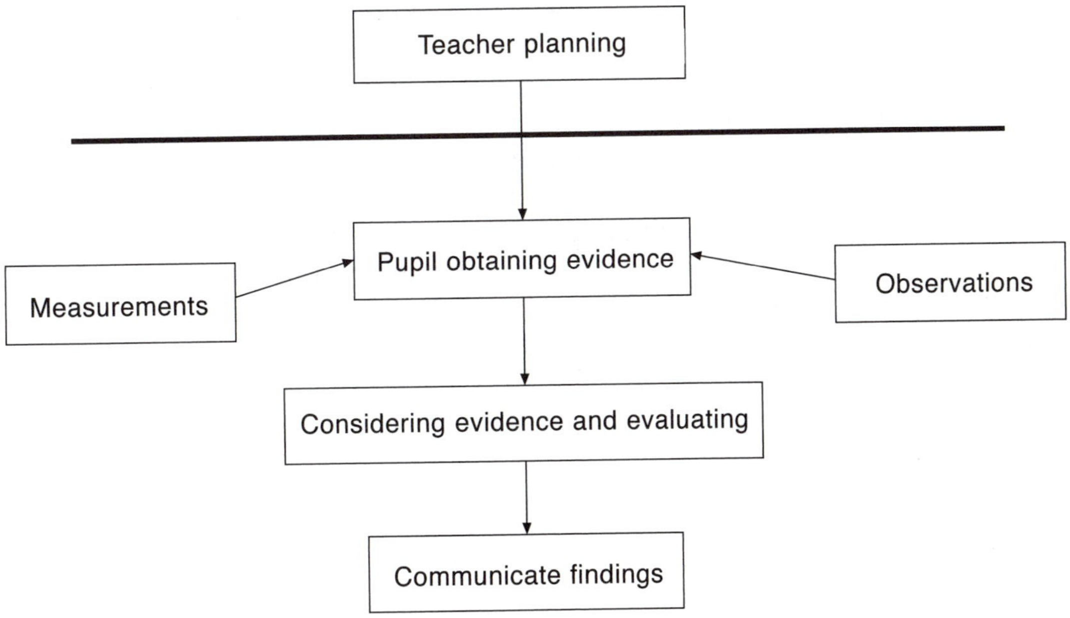

Figure 4.5 Illustrative work

to a great extent what children will do, observe, measure and record. Illustrative practicals consolidate particular skills and highlight concepts.

In this type of activity the children are told exactly what to do and what to observe, hence there is no box for pupil planning in Figure 4.5. The point of the practical is to illustrate a particular scientific principle or concept. For example, an irreversible change can be demonstrated by the pupils baking a cake. A more dramatic demonstration of such a change is achieved by the teacher burning a sheet of newspaper.

In another example of an illustrative practical, children are asked to build different shaped pillars from single pieces of A4 paper and test to see which is the strongest by placing weights on them. The different shapes are already drawn for them on a pro forma and they will find that a cylinder is the strongest. This could then be related to other contexts (bones, plant stems) where cylinders are used for support. In this case, the teacher has planned a fair test for the pupils and told them exactly how to carry out the practical work.

The evidence obtained can be analysed and conclusions drawn, with the help of the teacher's eliciting questions and hence challenge and the encouragement of higher order thinking can be incorporated in this type of practical.

Investigative work

The area below the line in Figure 4.1 illustrates the processes involved in investigative work. Goldsworthy and Feasey (1997) highlight the fact that one of the central features of an investigation is that you always change something and measure the effect it has on something else. This requires the planning of a fair test. This may be very simple, for example watering one plant and not another. It may be more complex, such as investigating factors that determine the brightness of a bulb. It is necessary to determine that effects observed are actually the result of the change and not something else or that the change would have happened anyway. Harlen (2001) calls this an action-testing investigation.

An extension of this is the finding of patterns in the way one thing changes as a result of changing another. For example, from observation of plants under and next to a hedgerow, children could look for patterns in plant height and light intensity. Another example is looking for patterns between the area of a parachute and the time taken to fall. This type of work involves higher order skills and the use of higher order thinking.

Scientific enquiry and higher order thinking skills

Investigative science has particular potential for providing challenge for able pupils because it provides ample opportunities for the use of higher order thinking skills. Research by Coates and Eyre (1999) and Coates and Wilson (2000) indicate that highly able scientists at the beginning of Key Stage 2 are capable of working at Level 4 in Attainment Target 1, Scientific enquiry. Similarly Year 6 children who are able scientists should have the skills to deal with the concepts associated with Level 6 within this part of the science curriculum. Tables 4.1 and 4.2 indicate the clear links between Attainment Target 1 of Curriculum 2000 (QCA/DfEE 1999) and higher order thinking skills.

Table 4.1 Links between Attainment Target 1 Level 4 and higher order thinking skills

Higher level thinking in Bloom's (1956) taxonomy	Scientific enquiry. Sc1/AT1 Level 4
Application	• Where appropriate, children can make predictions.
Analysis	• In their own investigative work, they decide on an appropriate approach to answer a question.
Synthesis	• They begin to relate conclusions to patterns in data and to scientific knowledge and understanding. • They describe or show in the way they perform their task, how to vary one factor while keeping others the same.
Evaluation	• Children can suggest improvements in their work, giving reasons.

Table 4.2 Links between Attainment Target 1 Level 6 and higher order thinking skills

Higher level thinking in Bloom's (1956) taxonomy	Scientific enquiry. Sc1/AT1 Level 6
Analysis	• In their own investigative work, children use scientific knowledge and understanding to identify an appropriate approach.
Synthesis	• Children draw conclusions that are consistent with the evidence and use scientific knowledge and understanding to explain them.
Evaluation	• Children make reasoned suggestions about how their working methods could be improved.

It has to be admitted that it is not an easy exercise to organise a whole class so that it is involved in meaningful investigations and, at the same time, to ensure that the able pupils are experiencing sufficient challenge. It is therefore possibly not surprising to note that Ofsted's Annual Report for 1997/8 indicates that the greatest variation in science teaching was in experimental and investigative science with highly able pupils being insufficiently challenged in some schools (Ofsted 1999). Again in 2001 Ofsted reported that 'high achieving pupils are still often given insufficiently challenging investigative work'. Various means of facilitating the planning of effective investigative work will therefore be considered in some detail.

The focus of the scientific enquiry

One means of facilitating this process is to concentrate the investigation on particular strands of Sc1 and to focus on areas that require higher order thinking. Goldsworthy and Feasey (1997) note that it is very important for children to have opportunities to combine all of their skills together in a complete investigation but point out that it is vital to consider each of these skills in turn through direct experience and teaching. It is essential therefore, sometimes, to support or scaffold able children through the various stages of an investigation.

It is often advantageous for teaching to be planned to focus on one part of a strand of Sc1, for example making predictions. Children need to be taught that a prediction in science should include a valid scientific reason which takes it beyond a guess. This involves children in applying their knowledge to a new situation. When presented with an investigation such as 'Can people with the strongest legs jump the furthest?' children will often state that people with the strongest legs can jump the furthest. When they are pressed to produce a scientific reason for this their argument often becomes circular, i.e. 'People with the strongest legs jump the furthest because they have the strongest legs.' This requires the judicious use of questions to draw out children's ideas to form a reasonable prediction. The reiteration of the question 'Why?' may produce answers such as 'They need stronger legs to overcome gravity.' This questioning process may take some time and it would then be appropriate for the teacher to support children more directly to plan and carry out the investigation.

Pupil grouping

It is often beneficial to group the able scientists together for the practical part of the lesson. This is particularly the case for scientific investigations so that the able pupils can work at their own pace and level of complexity. This may then mean that they will need less support in terms of the planning and carrying out of the investigation or, alternatively, more support if conducting a more complex investigation than the rest of the class.

Teacher questioning

It is, however, quite possible for pupils to become caught up in the doing of the investigation rather than in the thinking associated with it. As has been discussed in the previous chapter, the teacher's use of thought-provoking and probing questions is vital to maintaining a high level of challenge. O'Brien (1998) encourages teachers to question children, for example, about the purpose of their practical work and the spotting of relationships in their results. Hence investigations become enquiry orientated, as the concentration is on the analysis of data, evaluation of properties and/or synthesis of ideas, i.e. areas that require higher order thinking.

Considering data

The QCA report *Standards at Key Stage 2, English, mathematics and science* (2000) noted that since 1995, children generally succeeded on questions in the SAT papers which required them to read data from bar charts, graphs or tables. However, children were less successful on items that required interpretation of that data. This is hardly surprising because, as can be seen in Tables 4.1 and 4.2, children need to use the higher order thinking skill of synthesis to achieve this.

Interpreting data is one of the skills that able children have the potential to use, but direct teaching and practice of this is necessary for its development. There are a number of ways of achieving this without the pupils always needing to go through the full investigative process themselves in order to obtain data which can then be analysed. This might include examining data from other children in the class or from other secondary sources. The concept of skill development within Sc1 is a feature of the old and new Ginn *STAR Science Series* (Feasey *et al.* 2001) and there are photocopiable resources, which give pupils the opportunity to interrogate and analyse existing data. Goldsworthy *et al.* (2000a) have also concentrated on this in their publication, *Investigations: Developing understanding*. Among other things, this gives the pupils opportunities to criticise other (fictitious) pupils' interpretation of data. Being human, it is fun to criticise and this turns that trait to good use.

Variables

We can develop the complexity and hence the difficulty of an investigation by changing the type of variables under investigation. There are three types of variables which primary children will need to use and there is a clear progression in their level of complexity. These three types of variables are:

1. **Categoric** variables are descriptive or a classification: for example, the different types of magnet or the colour of a flower.

2. **Discrete** variables are numerical, but take only whole numbers or integers: for example, the number of layers of insulation around a can of water or the number of seeds that germinate.
3. **Continuous** variables are also numerical but can take any value: for example, length, weight, volume, time and temperature.

We can illustrate these variables by examining an investigation involving parachutes. After a period of open exploration, play and discussion children could be involved in the following investigations:

1. Which type of material makes the best parachute? (Categoric variables.) Children can make parachutes out of different textiles or paper and drop them at the same time to see which stays in the air the longest. Children can draw a bar chart from their data.
2. How does increasing the number of paper clips hanging from the parachute, affect the time of descent? (Discrete variables.) Children will use one parachute and therefore need to time its descent to the floor with different numbers of paper clips attached. Children can again draw a bar chart from their data.
3. How does the area of the parachute affect the time of descent? (Continuous variables.) Children will need to make parachutes with the same shape but different areas. They will then time their descent to the floor. Children can plot a line graph because the data consists of two continuous variables.

At the start of Key Stage 2 children can be involved in this type of investigation and the able pupils are capable of dealing with discrete or continuous variables, such as examples 2 and 3. This might involve guidance from the teachers to steer children in that direction. We would not necessarily expect them to draw line graphs at this stage, however, but later in Key Stage 2 they should also be guided to use continuous variables, when appropriate, and then display their data in line graphs. This gives them opportunities to describe patterns in their data and link this to their scientific knowledge and understanding.

Drawing graphs can be a laborious process and it is one which can be enhanced and facilitated by the use of ICT. Software packages, such as the spreadsheet NUMBER MAGIC (RM 2000) are well suited to this purpose. NUMBER MAGIC is available from Research Machines plc, New Mill House, 183 Milton Park, Abingdon OX14 4SE, Tel: 0870 9200200.

Degrees of openness

A further method of developing investigations and using them to differentiate is the degree of openness exhibited by the task. There are three features of a science investigation that can be viewed in terms of how closed or open they are. This is illustrated in Table 4.3 (Jones *et al.* 1992).

Table 4.3 Features that determine the degree of openness in a science investigation (*Source*: Jones *et al.* 1992)

Defining the problem	
Closely defined →	Not defined
Variables specified →	Variables not specified
Choosing a method	
Teacher tells pupils what to do →	Free choice of method
Arriving at solutions	
One acceptable solution →	Many acceptable solutions

The following examples of investigations illustrate the ideas.

Investigation A. Make cylindrical, cuboid and prism-shaped pillars from the same-sized pieces of card. Investigate which shape is the strongest by placing weights on them until they can hold no more.

Investigation B. Find out which shape of pillar will hold the greatest weight.

Investigation C. Investigate the factors that affect the strength of pillars.

Investigation A is closed in all areas. The variables are defined, the children are told what to do and one solution is expected, the cylindrical pillar will be the strongest. Investigation B is more open than investigation A. The variables are defined but the children need to decide which shapes to investigate how they will carry out the investigation. In investigation C no variables are specified and this task is therefore the most open of the three. The more open the investigation is the more decisions the child needs to make and these are clearly related to the higher order thinking skills outlined in Tables 4.1 and 4.2. Able children at the start of Key Stage 2 need to be involved in investigations in which at least one area is open, similar to investigation B. This investigation will involve the children in the skills of analysis and synthesis if they are to decide on an appropriate method and perform a fair test and give them access to Level 4 in Attainment Target 1. By the end of Key Stage 2 the able children should sometimes be involved in investigating where all three aspects are open. Again this will involve the higher order thinking skills of analysis and synthesis and access to Level 6.

5 Sc2 Life processes and living things

Life processes

QCA units (DfEE/QCA 1998): 3A Teeth and eating; 4A Moving and growing; 4B Habitats; 5A Keeping healthy; 5B Life cycles; 6A Interdependence and adaptation

The concepts involved in life processes obviously will be discussed in most units of work associated with living things. Hence the number of QCA units referenced here.

It can be a real challenge to decide what is living or non-living, and to explain the reasons behind these decisions, as this involves an understanding of life processes. Because of the number of QCA units of work which mention part of this strand, the basic understanding as to how we know whether or not something is alive can be overlooked. It is our contention that whenever living things are discussed, it is beneficial to reinforce these fundamental ideas of life processes.

Bright ideas

> **Living or non-living?**
>
> The pupils are given a set of items and they need to decide which category they fall into. The level of challenge will be high if some of the following items are included: a piece of wood, a fossil, a cut flower, a shell, a feather, a potato, a nut and a seed.

The pupils can work in groups to consider the items and then bring their ideas together as a whole class. The question is likely to cause controversy. It makes sense, at this time, to widen the discussion by creating three categories:

Alive, once alive, never alive?

It is a common misconception to consider a seed, a nut and a potato as 'once alive'. In fact they are still living and can grow into plants. They are dormant, alive but not actively growing, and can be shown to be respiring, albeit slowly. The wood, shell and feather were all once part of a living thing and therefore they were once alive. The fossil could be the remains of a plant or animal and therefore was once living but it could be simply evidence that an animal or plant was once there – footprints or an impression in the rock. Is a cut flower alive? At which point does death occur? Basically the cells in the flower start to die from the point of severance, but you cannot identify at which precise point it is dead as this is a gradual process.

This work can be developed into an odd one out activity, including any of the items in the list, for example:

A shell, a plant and a rock

Which is the odd one out?

Among the many possible answers are:

- The shell because it was a part of an animal.
- The plant because it is living.
- The rock because it has never been alive (as long as it does not contain fossils).

Is a flame alive?

A flame appears to exhibit many of the life processes:

- Nutrition – it uses fuel
- Growth – fires become larger
- Movement – flames flicker
- Reproduction – flames can leap from one place to another
- It produces 'waste' – ash and smoke
- It needs oxygen.

Of course, a flame is not living as it is not made up of cells and it is not growing, reproducing or producing waste in a biological sense. This can form the basis of a very interesting discussion.

Pupils as researchers

A section of the website, QUEST, from the Natural History Museum of London, is particularly useful for challenging able children:

http://www.nhm.ac.uk/education/quest2/english/whyquest.html

QUEST stands for Questioning, Understanding and Exploring Simulated Things. It provides images of objects, such as a pollen grain or a skull, and allows children to make virtual observations, such as the weight and size, and allows them to view the object from all sides. There is a section that allows children to ask scientists for advice on better questions and a notebook to record and share observations. This website will help children to develop many of the scientific skills associated with investigations and encourage the use of higher level thinking skills.

Humans and other animals

QCA units (DfEE/QCA 1998) : 3A Teeth and eating; 4A Moving and growing; 5A Keeping healthy; 5B Life cycles; 6B Micro-organisms

Bright ideas

Which is the odd one out?

Playing odd one out is an ideal way to extend children's thinking about all aspects of humans and other animals. They can be given pictures of:

- a worm, a snake and a centipede
- the skeletons of a fish, a bird and a dog
- an insect, a snail and a frog.

(http://www.yahooligans.com will provide website links for these pictures.)

In this activity there are no correct answers. What is expected is that children can give clear, reasoned arguments to support their ideas. It is in fact possible to select each one as the odd one out. For example:

- The worm is the only one that lives under the ground, eats soil and decaying vegetation and cannot see. The snake (generally) and centipede can both see and are carnivores.
- The snake is the only vertebrate – it has an internal skeleton. Unlike the other two it does not have a segmented body.
- The centipede is the only one with legs and feelers.

This exercise may provide an incentive for the pupils to undertake some research to find out more about these animals. They can then return to the odd one out activity to refine their reasoning with an increased depth of understanding.

Pupils as researchers

London Zoo has an interactive website (http://www.weboflife.co.uk/weboflife/species_web/index.html), which is based on the Web of Life exhibit. There are quizzes for children to try to identify animals and there are species searches. Children can investigate the characteristics of various species and perhaps find out why some species are now endangered. They can use the information in a presentation or to develop quizzes for the rest of the class.

The CD-ROM *The Ultimate Human Body* (Dorling Kindersley 1994) can be used to challenge children by allowing them to investigate topics at a greater depth. For example, the children can investigate how the heart and circulatory systems work. They can then feed back this information to the rest of the class in an innovative way. They may use ICT and develop a PowerPoint presentation. They will need to use evaluation skills firstly to set out criteria for the information they are wanting to present and secondly to judge what information is relevant and why.

More complex relationships can be explored to increase the depth of study, for example:

How do joints help the body move?

How are birds or fish skeletons adapted for flying or swimming?

How does your body stay upright when you move?

The following sites are useful sources for all of these questions:

www.learn.co.uk/default.asp?WCI=Unit&WCU=8533
www.digitalbrain.com/digitalbrain/web/subjects/1.%20primary/ks2sci/sc2/execise3.db_psc
http://www.eskeletons.org/

Teeth

Examining animals' skulls and trying to draw conclusions about diet can be an interesting research activity. Many schools will not have a collection for children to examine but the website http://www.calacademy.org/exhibits/skulls/diversity.html has a host of skulls with different teeth for the pupils to consider.

Mummy's teeth tell all!

This can be extended to research into humans and the relationship between teeth, diet and lifestyle. One way of doing this is to study Egyptian mummies (http://www.toledmuseum.org/learnMore_mummy.html) to find out what can be learnt about the state of their teeth and whether they suffered from decay.

Find the Golden Ratio

Children can investigate their own bodies to find out the relationships between the sizes of different parts of the body. The ancient Greeks took body measurements and found that the same ratio kept appearing. They called it the Golden Ratio, which is 1.61:1. The website http://www.geocities.com/CapeCanaveral/Station/8228/ gives more information about this.
The ASE SY Primary CD-ROM (Association for Science Education 2002) has an activity, which examines 'Golden Ratios'. Children are required to measure:

- the width of an eye
- the width of the bridge of the nose
- the width of their whole smile
- the width of teeth we can see when you smile.

They are then required to divide the bridge of the nose width by the eye width and the mouth width by the teeth width and compare the ratios for themselves and other members of the class. Again this will be aided by the use of a spreadsheet, such as EXCEL. It is fascinating to discover how often the number obtained approximates to the Golden Ratio.

Children can carry out research into how this ratio influenced building design, for example the Parthenon and more contemporary designs, which contain the same shapes that can be seen in Greek temples. This can be facilitated using a search engine (http://www.yahooligans.com) or pictures from books and magazines.

Find other ratios

Not all measurements lead to the Golden Ratio. Pupils can investigate the links between head length and the total body length for people of different ages. They may need the cooperation of other members of staff and pupils, and contact with families who have babies to get a complete picture. If the total body length is divided by the head length for adults, the answer will be about six, but for children it will be smaller as their heads are larger in comparison to their bodies.

Investigations

Investigate pulse rates

Within the QCA Scheme of Work (5A Keeping healthy), children are expected to investigate the pulse rates of different members of the class, and follow this up with an activity that examines the effect of exercise on pulse rate. This will involve the children in manipulating the continuous variables, for example the timing of the exercise, and making decisions about the method they will use to obtain data. One activity within this unit asks children to 'speculate about factors which could change the pulse rate'. Children are expected to give reasons for their opinions, which are deduced from experimental data and other evidence available, and finally to explain how they have developed their ideas. This can be developed further so that children investigate whether there is any connection between pulse rate and breathing rate. They will need to devise a test to compare pulse and breathing rates of people in different situations, for example lying down, standing or after running on the spot.

The data can be entered into a spreadsheet and plotted in a scattergram to check if there is a connection. This investigation will involve the children in manipulating more than one variable and making decisions about the methods that they use to obtain data. Once the two sets of data have been obtained, the pupils will be able to decide if they are connected and then come up with a theory as to why or why not this is the case.

Physical fitness and the aspects of life associated with this comprise a second area that can be developed within these units.

Do the people with the strongest legs jump the furthest?

This is an excellent opportunity to concentrate on one element of Sc1, prediction. The pupils will need to decide how to measure strength of legs and there are various ways of doing this. It is possible to place a set of bathroom scales vertically against a wall and then allow a child to push against them. This will give a measurement which relates to the size of the push. This measurement will be in kilograms and a push should be measured in Newtons but the larger the push, the larger the reading on the scale and so the two are directly related. Alternatively, the pupils may decide on another method for measuring strength, one group of children decided that the width of the thigh gives a measure of strength!

It will be very important to explain to the children that a scientific prediction needs an explanation, hence they will need to record it in the form:

'I think . . . because . . .'

It is likely that the children will initially produce a circular argument, such as 'I think that the people with the strongest legs will jump the furthest because they have the strongest legs.' Keep asking them 'Why?' until they draw on their existing scientific understanding.

Do people with the longest stride length run 100 m the fastest?

This is an alternative investigation. It will require the pupils to make predictions, decide how to carry out a fair test in the investigation and compare their findings with the prediction. Their results can be displayed in a cross and line graph.

Who is fit?

Devising tests to assess physical fitness and trying them out on a group in the class will increase the complexity of the investigative work even further. This investigation is completely open. The children will need to define what they understand by the term 'fit', decide which variables to control, which to change and which to measure and hence devise their own investigations. Alternative solutions to the investigation are likely to arise, as different groups of children will be working on alternative ideas about fitness.

This can be followed up with comparisons made between the experimental data and people's own perceptions of their own fitness. Again the children will have to decide on their own theories to determine any links between sets of data. They would have brought in their own knowledge to help explain the links.

Pupils can be asked to investigate the relationships between a series of variables:

Is there a link between your weight and how high you can jump?

Is there a link between how tall you are and how high you can jump?

In each of the above investigations, pupils need to stand against a wall and reach up as high as they can. This is measured and is their reach height. They can then perform a standing jump to see how far up the wall they can touch. This is also measured and the difference between the two is the jump height.

Are there any other relationships?

The emphasis is on looking for patterns in data, to examine relationships between sets of data and to think of a theory to link them together. This is an ideal opportunity for the pupils to use a software package, such as NUMBER MAGIC (RM 2000) to display their findings so that conclusions can be drawn from their findings.

The activity can be related to real life by asking the pupils to identify the characteristics a high jump coach would look for in people she or he was selecting to train. Children can be given pictures of high jumpers from sports magazines and relate these to their own findings.

Green plants

QCA units (DfEE/QCA 1998): 3B Helping plants grow well; 5B Life cycles; 6A Interdependence and adaptation

Examining the optimum conditions for plant growth and seed germination are science investigations, which are very popular in school. The science curriculum states that children should be taught about 'the effects of light, water and temperature on plant growth'. These concepts are gradually developed through the three units. There tends to be some repetition of ideas that the more able children may already know and understand. A concept map to complete can be used to assess the pupils' understanding. If it is considered appropriate, it is then possible to compact the work, in that the able pupils do not need to revisit these concepts for any length of time and so can be given alternative tasks. Using a concept map also highlights any gaps in the children's knowledge.

Bright ideas

There are some very big ideas behind these concepts and asking the following questions can challenge children's thinking:

I planted a tree in my garden four years ago. It now weighs 250 kg more. Where did this 250 kg come from?

It is amazing to consider the fact that the mass of the tree has been produced as a result of photosynthesis. Pupils at Key Stage 2 are not expected to understand the concept of photosynthesis but they are expected to understand 'the role of the leaf in producing new material for growth'. It is a common misconception among children and adults to think that the roots take in the food for the plant and this is not helped by the fact that some fertilisers are labelled 'plant food'. The roots take in the necessary minerals but the green plant makes its own 'food' (sugar) in its leaves using the Sun's energy which is captured in the leaves and carbon dioxide (from the air) and water (from the ground). The pupils therefore need to understand that the light and water and air (the carbon dioxide) are necessary for growth because the leaf 'processes' these to form the mass of the plant.

Why do bluebells flower in the woods in springtime and not later in the year?

The bluebells flower before the leaf canopy has been established and so there is enough light for them to grow effectively.

Why do some seeds remain dormant until spring?

The required conditions for growth are not available until the warmer weather.

Why do ferns produce poisons that prevent plants from growing close to them?

This results in them having no competition for the light and water.

Why do seaweeds like Bladder wrack have air sacs on their fronds?

When the tide is in the air sacs or bladders keep the fronds near the surface of the water where it is light enough for them to photosynthesise.

How can we get strawberries in December?

It is likely that this discussion will centre on the necessary conditions for the growth of strawberry plants and how these can be simulated in the winter. The use of a greenhouse, artificial light and heat sources will need to be considered.

Pupils as researchers

Should genetically engineered food crops be specially labelled for consumers and why?

This research question is taken from the ASE SY Primary CD-ROM (Association for Science Education 2002) WEBSEARCH section, DNA for Dinner (http://www.gis.net/%7Epeacewp/webquest.htm). The site offers children the opportunity to undertake a WebQuest: 'The site provides information and links to other sites to help children develop their own ideas about this subject.' The site is heavily biased towards use in the USA, for instance it asks the children to e-mail Congress with their report and ideas. But this can easily be replaced by e-mailing their local MP.

Problem solving

Grow a virtual plant

Children can grow a virtual plant by downloading one from:

http://www.desksoft.com/DesktopPlant.htm

They have the option of varying the amount of water, light, temperature and fertiliser it receives. From this activity they can discover the optimum conditions necessary for plant growth and use this to check their own experimental findings.

Investigations

Investigations can focus on whether plants need light and warmth or a given amount of water for healthy growth. The majority of children in the class can have closed investigations where the teacher defines the problem and method for the children. For example, they can compare the growth of two sets of cress seedlings: one set in a dark cupboard and another set in the light. Alternatively, they can vary the amount of water a plant receives, while keeping all other variables constant. However, the able children can be given a much more open investigation, such as 'What affects plant growth?' This will mean that they have to devise their own method for the investigation.

If the able children have a clear understanding of the conditions for plant growth they can be grouped together to develop investigations which increase the breadth and depth of their understanding, as in the following examples.

Is soil really necessary?

It is possible to investigate plant growth in various substrates – cotton wool, sawdust, pads of foam rubber, new and used tea bags. Cress seedlings would be suitable for this investigation. Observations can be made, such as when leaves, roots and shoots appear and the length of the plants can be measured. They can investigate the effects of fertiliser on the plants that became unhealthy.

Do plants need leaves to grow well?

The children will need to decide what they are going to measure, what they are going to change and what they will keep the same, i.e. how to make it a fair test. This will involve the children in removing leaves from a number of plants. One of the features of the discussion at the end is likely to be the need for a very large number of plants to obtain reliable data. Bean seedlings would be suitable for this investigation.

Variation and classification

QCA units (DfEE/QCA 1998): 4B Habitats; 6A Interdependence and adaptation

Pupils as researchers

Pupils can carry out research to examine various relationships between the shape of an animal's body and its environment, for example:

What is the relationship between a bird's beak and its food?

What is the relationship between a bird's feet and the habitat in which it lives?

A good site to carry out this research is:
http://education.leeds.ac.uk/~edu/technology/epb97/forest/k_feet.htm

Steady on their feet

Pupils can undertake practical research into why some animals have splayed-out legs. Plasticine animals can be made with one leg at each 'corner'. The legs can be made from straws with a plasticine foot. The models can have legs of varying lengths and different amounts of splay. The model animals can be placed on a slope, which is raised until the animal falls over. A more stable animal will stay upright on a steeper slope.

They can support any conclusions or develop initial hypotheses by carrying out research into actual animals, such as giraffes, and the splay of their legs. Animals with longer legs tend to splay them out for increased stability.

Living things in their environment

QCA units (DfEE/QCA 1998): 4B Habitats; 6A Interdependence and adaptation; 6B Micro-organisms

Bright ideas

Pupils' thinking and reasoning can be challenged by questioning them about the links in a food chain. For example:

Green plan → snail → thrush → cat

- Why do thrushes still exist in spite of cats?
- What would happen if all of the snails died?
- Snails love warm wet summers. What would happen in a summer like that?

Critical thinking about a specific scenario will extend pupils' thinking and the following problem is taken from an idea by Robert Swartz (2002).

Foxes and rabbits

- When rabbits are near farms, they eat the farmer's crops. Farmers have killed thousands of rabbits because of this. Foxes eat rabbits. Explain what problems this poses for foxes and why they are problems.
- Can you think of any ways that people can save foxes and still control rabbits? Explain what you might do. What would you have to do in order to make sure your solution works? Is there anything you already know that has a bearing on this?
- Suppose you were asked to observe the feeding habits of foxes so that you could gather some data about the problem. Describe what you would do to make sure that your observations were as accurate as possible and that you brought back data that other people could trust. Write a plan listing all the things you would think about beforehand.

Pupils' ideas can be challenged by asking them to describe how the human body has adapted to help us survive. The following questions will stimulate children's thinking:

How has the human body adapted to help it survive?

The work can be extended to allow the children to think about adaptations that have not yet happened to allow humans to cater for different environments or access different environments, for example:

What could we do if we had a skeleton made out of a flexible material or even have no skeleton at all?

How could we adapt to live under the sea as well as on the land?

Hot seating

The strand which deals with micro-organisms can be deepened by research into harmful disease-causing microbes and the ways we have developed to combat them. Pupils can research Jenner or Pasteur, using books or the Internet, and then be hot seated by the rest of the class.

Pupils as researchers

Investigate different environments

The children can investigate an environment, which is completely different from their own, for example:

- http://passporttoknowledge.com has a link called 'Live from the rainforest'.
- http://www.field-guides.com has links to a variety of environments, for example, mountains and under the sea.
- http://www.bbc.co.uk/education/landmarks is a website that examines the changes human population increases have had on five different environments.

They can carry out research into adaptations to climate or habitats that they would not normally encounter. For the habitat they choose to investigate they can answer some of the following questions:

What are the features of the habitat?

What organisms are found in the habitat?

What specialised adaptations did any organism have?

Why are these adaptations important for the organism's survival?

What adaptations did any organisms have in common?

What do you think are the three most important adaptations?

Why do you think they are important?

Children can carry out research into cholera:

What is cholera?

One of the aims of this project will be to introduce the pupils to the nature of urban life in nineteenth-century Britain and to make links to modern knowledge about disease and infection. The research can be enhanced using the Pfizer Fun Zone on the Internet (http://www.pfizerfunzone.com). In the 'Time Machine' section children can travel back in time and discover the effects medicine and disease have had in history.

In the following questions the pupils are asked to suggest answers to some puzzling questions from nature and they can then carry out research to discover the accuracy of their suggestions:

How do you think arctic fish are adapted to live in sea water that is below the freezing point of their bodies?

Their bodies contain anti-freeze.

Why is this an important adaptation?

Find out how alligators can see underwater?

They have a third sideways eyelid which still lets them see.

Why is this an important adaptation?

In each of the above cases, a Google advanced search will produce a wealth of associated websites.

Problem solving

Children are required to understand food chains and feeding relationships. Able children's work can be given breadth by asking them to:

Make a food web for a particular environment.

This can be done by giving them a number of food chains and asking them to construct a food web. The website http://education.leeds.ac.uk/~edu/technology/epb97/forest/fdwb.htm has an example of a food web that can be used by the teacher to pick out food chains. The pupils can then construct a food web from these chains. There will be many other sites which can be accessed by a search engine.

Investigations

The unit from the QCA Scheme of Work, 5/6H Enquiry in environmental and technological contexts gives opportunities for challenging children and developing their evaluation skills. They are expected to carry out research into factors affecting dandelions' growth in two different locations. The expectations for able children state that they will 'plan what to do and how to use available resources effectively; suggest limitations of the data collected . . . and how these could be reduced' (QCA/DFEE 2000). They will be making critical judgements about their data and developing confidence in these judgements.

The Natural History Museum, London organises opportunities for children to take part in nationwide scientific studies through the Internet. The 2000 investigation was called 'Walking with woodlice' (http://www.nhm.ac.uk/woodlice/page006.html) and set out to build up a UK database after children had investigated their local environment and sent in their data.

What factors affect the growth of yeast?

When studying micro-organisms pupils can set up their own investigation into the best conditions for yeast growth.

For yeast to grow effectively, it needs to be mixed with sugar and warm water. As it grows, it produces carbon dioxide. If the mixture is placed in a test tube or a narrow jar with a balloon over the end, the balloon will inflate as the carbon dioxide is produced.

The pupils can investigate how varying the temperature or the amount of sugar changes the amount of carbon dioxide produced. They can then be given some yeast, which has been baked, to develop the investigation further. The baking process kills the yeast and so no carbon dioxide is produced. This will cause a return to the discussion of life processes.

6 Sc3 Materials and their properties

Grouping and classifying materials

QCA units (DfEE/QCA 1998): 3C Characteristics of materials; 3D Rocks and soils; 4C Keeping warm; 4F Circuits and conductors; 5C Gases all around us; 5D Changing state

Bright ideas

The most challenging section of this part of the curriculum states that pupils are expected 'to recognise differences between solids, liquids and gases, in terms of ease of flow and maintenance of shape and volume' (QCA/DfEE 1999).

It is probably easiest to begin considering just solids and liquids. Our brains are wonderful things and we do not find it difficult to recognise a liquid when we see one or a solid when we bump into one! However, it is much more difficult to define, or put into words, what is meant by a solid or a liquid. It is a real challenge to accurately define the recognition process, which our brain performs almost instantly. This can be the source of a most fascinating discussion with children.

Describe a solid and describe a liquid

The children can be shown a selection of materials and asked whether they are solids or liquids. This should include a wide variety of materials with varying properties. Children find it easy to spot water, vinegar and oil as liquids and bricks, sponges and chalk as solids. They can then be asked to describe the properties of a liquid and how they are different from that of a solid. They will often describe a liquid as wet but what exactly does wet mean? They will tend to say that you can 'put your hand through a liquid' but then I can put my hand through sand in a sandpit. They will describe a solid as hard and can then be shown a sponge and asked if that is then a liquid.

This discussion can be used to encourage metacognition if it is pointed out that we tend to recognise quickly which materials are liquids and which are solids but we find it very hard to pin down how our brain carries out this categorisation. Hence, perhaps rather crudely, we are encouraging the children to think about their thinking.

Children tend to be able to arrive, with pertinent questioning and prompting from the teacher, at the concept of a solid having a fixed shape while a liquid will take the shape of its container. This may well lead them to point out that sand or flour will take the shape of its container. However, of course, one grain of sand will have a fixed shape.

In scientific terms, the definitions can be made short and sharp:

- a **solid** has a fixed volume and a fixed shape;
- a **liquid** has a fixed volume and no fixed shape;
- a **gas** has no fixed volume or shape.

Primary children can struggle with the concept of a gas and often associate it solely with a source of heat for cooking. As it is not possible to bring any of the coloured gases, such as chlorine and bromine, into the primary school this can prove rather problematic. It is obviously not possible to see air but it is possible to see its effects, such as feeling the pressure when a finger is placed over the end of a bicycle pump and the piston is pushed in. A perfume bottle can be opened at the front of the class and children experience the fact that the gas spreads out to fill the container, in this case the room. They may well have experienced this more unpleasantly with a stink bomb. It is then possible to enter into an extension of the previous discussion and consider the characteristics of solids, liquids and gases.

As has been said, the children may well notice that a heap of sand will take the shape of its container and, in this way, it behaves like a liquid. The ball pool that is common in children's soft play areas is another example of this. At least one mother (one of the authors) has had to be restrained from diving in to rescue her child who disappeared under the balls in a ball pool, because the appearance was so similar to drowning! This may lead on to a very big idea, which is called kinetic theory. Over the years, there has been some debate as to whether primary children should be introduced to the idea of the existence of atoms. It seems such a shame to deprive bright young children of the opportunity to enjoy this big idea. This is obviously an extension activity as it goes beyond the Key Stage 2 curriculum.

Atoms – a thought experiment

Children can be introduced fairly simply to the idea of atoms by considering the process by which the ancient Greeks arrived at an understanding of their existence. This takes the form of a 'thought experiment'. The children can be asked to imagine a block of, for example, pure copper. If this is cut in half, there will be half a block of copper; if it is then cut in half again, a quarter will remain, then an eighth and so on and so on. Eventually, a point will be reached where the smallest piece remains that is still copper and this is the copper atom. This is obviously impossible practically and hence it is solely a thought experiment, an exercise in philosophy. However, children do tend to be able to follow this process.

As a class, act being a solid, a liquid and then a gas.

Kinetic theory is about the behaviour of atoms or groups of atoms joined together to form molecules and this can be acted out by groups of children. In solids, the atoms are closely held together and they cannot exchange their neighbours, they have some energy but just enough to 'jiggle' a bit. When they are given more energy, they can break away from their neighbours and move around but they are still fairly close together – hence they can flow and pour. Given even more energy, they fly off in all directions and so spread out as a gas. The teacher can act the role of a heater giving more energy.

Pupils are asked to consider the use of materials in terms of their properties and PMIs lend themselves well to considering this aspect of the curriculum.

PMI: Consider the positives, minuses and interesting points associated with one of these scenarios:

An umbrella made from glass

A house made of steel

A car made from plastic

Other aspects of this strand involve children in classifying materials by examining their properties.

What's my material?

Children can be asked to describe a material, such as leather or glass, without mentioning its name to the rest of the group (class) in such a way as the others can guess what it is.

What is a good material for a saucepan handle and why?

Saucepan handles tend to be made of plastic or wood as these materials do not conduct the heat and so the pan can be picked up without risk of burning. The pupils can look at different saucepans and decide which ones can only be picked up when wearing oven gloves. Antique silver teapots often have an ivory ring between the body of the pot and the handle so that it is insulated.

The game 'odd one out' lends itself particularly to this section of the syllabus, as the pupils will tend to draw naturally on the properties of the materials for their reasons. An example of this is given in Chapter 2, 'Chocolate, paper and water – which is the odd one out?' The following are further suggestions:

Which is the odd one out?

- Sand, iron filings and sawdust
- Glass, lemonade and water
- Three different types of rocks

> **If you were choosing rock for a statue, which would you choose?**
>
> This can be used as a discussion before the properties of rocks have been studied and can then provide a focus for subsequent investigations.

Concept cartoons

As in all the other areas of the science curriculum, the concept cartoons of Naylor and Keogh (2000) are well suited to the discussion of ideas and concepts, for example cartoon 8.5 'Liquids' would be appropriate here.

Pupils as researchers

The study of rocks is an ideal subject for children to carry out their own research. The BBC website (http://www.bbc.co.uk/education/rocks/index.shtml) contains a wealth of accessible information, including animations.

Rocks are chosen for a particular purpose because of their characteristics. Two websites that have rich sources of ideas and information related to this are:

http://www.rocksforkids.com/index.html
http://www.sdnhm.org/kids/minerals/index.html

Another website that links to many other related sites is:

http://directory.google.com/Top/Science/Earth_Sciences/Geology/Rocks_and_Minerals/Education

Problem solving

Interestingly when drops of water are spilled onto a piece of newspaper, the water spreads out to form an oval shape and not a circle.

> **Why does water form an oval, and not a circle, when it is absorbed by newspaper?**
>
> If a torn newspaper is examined with a hand lens, it is possible to see the fibres of wood going in one direction. The water flows more easily along the fibres and hence the oval shape.

The activity can be extended into an investigation to consider the strength of the paper.

Is newspaper as strong in each direction?

The pupils can devise an experiment to test the strength of newspaper along the fibres and across the fibres and relate their findings to the structure of the paper. Tearing the paper will allow the children to see how the fibres lie with a hand lens. One way of testing strength is to cut the paper into strips and to hang weights from a bulldog clip attached to the end until the paper breaks. Another way is to loop the paper through an elastic band and pull the band until the paper snaps. If the band is held alongside a ruler, it is possible to obtain a simple measure of the force required to break it, i.e. the longer the elastic band the greater the force.

Investigations

The snowman's coat

The snowman's coat can be a springboard for an investigation. The pupils are asked to design an investigation to find out how the coat affects the rate of melting. This involves the pupils in realising that they can model the behaviour of a real snowman and a coat by using ice cubes and a material. Some pupils may be tempted to try to build a snowman from the ice cubes!

In fact, what will happen to the snowman will depend on the air temperature. If the air temperature is above freezing, then the coat will reduce heat flow from the warmer air to the snowman and he will last longer. If the air temperature is below freezing, then the coat will not make much difference. The misconception that some people have is that the snowman will melt more quickly with the coat on. This relates to the fact that we wear coats in the winter to keep us warm and it can seem that they are providing heat. In practice, the coat acts as an insulator and reduces heat flow from our warm bodies to the cooler outside air. In the snowman, the coat again acts as an insulator and reduces heat flow from the warmer air to the colder snow.

Is it true that large penguins keep warmer than small penguins?

This is another problem that can be investigated by modelling a real-life situation. One way of doing this is to investigate the cooling of different volumes of hot water. A large volume of water will cool down to room temperature slower than a small volume.

Which melts faster – an ice cube or an iceberg?

Balloons filled with water placed in the freezer will produce very large blocks of ice. Their rate of melting can be compared with that of smaller ice cubes.

How can we keep the teacher's tea warm on playground duty?

This situation can be modelled, for example, by an investigation into the effect of different numbers of layers of insulating material around a jar of hot water. The temperature can be measured with a thermometer at intervals and then a graph plotted from the data collected. It is appropriate to use an ICT package here, such as EXCEL or NUMBER MAGIC (RM 2000) to plot the graph. Alternatively, a temperature sensor can be connected to the computer and then the graph can be plotted automatically. The graphs obtained with different layers of insulating material can be compared. The children may, however, decide to investigate the effect of different volumes of water, or having a lid on the mug.

Space suits are usually white. Why?

Pupils can carry out an investigation, which examines heating rather than cooling. This situation can be modelled by, for example, using three tin cans – shiny, painted white and painted matt black. Pupils will need to plan their own experiment but one method is to fill the cans with cold water and place them in front of an electric heater or in bright sunlight. The temperature of the water can then be recorded over a period of time. Once again this lends itself well to the use of a temperature sensor and data logging equipment but it can be done with the use of an ordinary thermometer. White is the poorest absorber of the radiation from the Sun, while black is the best. Hence, the white can will remain the coolest. If different coloured materials are spread on the ground on a hot, sunny day, it is possible to feel that black material becomes noticeably warmer than the white.

Which is the best paper towel?

Paper towels come in all colours and textures. This investigation can be presented as a consumer survey or as a practical means of helping the kitchen staff. The pupils will need to decide what is meant by the word, 'best'. There is a range of possible meanings that they can decide to investigate, such as the strength or the absorbency of the towels. Strength can be measured by placing weights on the different towels until they break; absorbency can be measured by placing the same size pieces of towel into beakers of water and weighing them before and after to see how much they have absorbed. The pupils may decide to drop water onto the towels and measure how far it spreads or cut strips and hang them into water and measure how far up the different towels the water travels. If they decide on this type of method, some higher order thinking is definitely required as it is not necessarily correct to assume that if the water spreads out further, the towel is more absorbent. It may be more absorbent if it spreads out less as a towel may then have a larger capacity for the water.

Which rock makes a good gravestone?

The BBC website (http://www.bbc.co.uk/education/rocks/rockcycle.shtml) contains some very interesting and stretching experiments with rocks that can be used with all the class to add spice and variety. For example, in experiment 3, Erosion, different rocks are placed safely in a plastic container with a lid and shaken to simulate the effect of weathering. Children can use the information gathered from this to decide which rocks would form high and low cliffs at the seaside or which would make hills and which valleys. They can decide which one of these rocks they would choose for a gravestone.

Changing materials

QCA units (DfEE/QCA 1998): 4C Keeping warm; 4D Solids, liquids and how they can be separated; 5C Gases all around us; 5D Changing state; 6D Reversible and irreversible changes

Bright ideas

> **Where does a puddle go?**
>
> This explores the process of evaporation and actually what is taking place, i.e. the change of state from a liquid to a gas.

Our understanding of chemical changes has only developed in comparatively recent times. The Greek idea that everything was made up of a combination of earth, water, air and fire was accepted truth for many years. As natural scientists began to examine the process of burning, they developed the Greek idea to come up with the substance phlogiston. The theory suggested that everything contained phlogiston and when burning this was released into the atmosphere. It was not until oxygen was discovered that this idea was refuted. Children's thinking and reasoning can be challenged by asking them to discuss alternative theories to a proposition, any limitations it might have and how they might convince people to change their ideas to the currently accepted explanation. They can consider the following proposition and develop arguments to refute it:

> **When flames consume wood, the fire is living because it needs air and it feeds on the wood.**

Pupils as researchers

As energy costs keep mounting and fossil fuel stocks diminish, there is a real need to conserve energy. Allowing heat energy to escape from gaps around doors and windows and through roofs that are not insulated is wasteful and expensive. It also results in extra heat energy being spread into the environment, which is one cause of global warming. This will become an increasingly vital issue. One way is to insulate our school and our homes more effectively.

> **Save the planet – insulate now!**
>
> Pupils can research into thermal insulation in the school and the home. This research can be practical by allowing them to do a survey of their school and home to discover the types of insulation being used. They can also make suggestions for possible improvements, such as keeping doors shut at playtime. This practical survey can be linked to research into the causes of global warming and the fossil fuel crisis. The website http://www.epa.gov/globalwarming/kids/gives child-friendly ideas about global warming and the greenhouse effect.

Problem solving

> **Stranded on a desert island – drinking water needed.**
>
> The pupils can be encouraged to come up with a scientific solution to this particular problem. The island will have no natural source of water so the pupils will need to devise a way of making sea water safe to drink. From their understanding of dissolving they can arrive at the idea of heating the sea water until it boils and then cooling the resulting water vapour so that pure water is collected. This process of evaporation and then condensation is called distillation. As this requires water to be boiled, they can only do this theoretically but they can be encouraged to design apparatus to do this from the types of natural materials likely to be found on a desert island.

Clean water is a major issue in the world today. The water supply in different parts of the world comes from different sources. This can be the basis of a piece of Internet research. The website http://www.dwi.gov.uk/pubs/private/#6 gives information about private water supplies and discusses how they can become contaminated. Children can use this information to examine issues from the website that relate to other parts of the world. The website http://www.epa.gov/safewater/protect/pdfs/swp_indian_fact. pdf provides information on drinking water quality in India.

A related topic is to carry out research into space travel. A spacecraft can only carry a limited amount of water.

> **How will the water supply be managed on a journey to Mars, which takes three years?**
>
> On space shuttle missions water from various sources is condensed, purified and recycled.

Investigations

Reversible changes involving melting ice can be used to develop investigations to challenge children's thinking. We all add ice to drinks to cool them down. This is the basis of the following work.

> **What happens to the temperature of water when we add ice to it?**
>
> Children can carry out an investigation which examines the effect of adding different numbers of ice cubes to the same volume of water. One ice cube is added to a given volume of tap water and the temperature measured after a certain time. This water is then thrown away and two ice cubes added to the same volume of tap water and the process repeated. This lends itself very well to the consideration of a fair test as the volume of water, the number of times it is stirred, the time the temperature is measured after the ice is added all need to be kept constant.
>
> This will give results which can be used to draw a bar chart and allow children to look for patterns in their data. As more cubes are added, the temperature will decrease and they can use the graph to predict what will happen when a certain number of ice cubes (more than those added in the practical) is added. One challenge for children is to realise that the temperature of the water cannot go below 0° C.
>
> The investigation can be varied by finding out what happens when one ice cube is added to different volumes of water.

Separating mixtures of materials

QCA units (DfEE/QCA 1998): 3D Rocks and soils; 4D Solids, liquids and how they can be separated; 6C More about dissolving; 6D Reversible and irreversible changes

Bright ideas

Where does the solid go when it dissolves?

When a solid dissolves, it appears to disappear but where has it gone? This can lead to the big idea of atoms as the solid breaks down into very, very small particles which are spread throughout the particles of the liquid. They are so small that they cannot be seen.

Pupils as researchers

We use techniques associated with separating mixtures of materials to extract minerals from the ground and to purify water. Examples of this can lead to pupils carrying out research in the following areas:

There are large deposits of salt under the ground in Cheshire. How did salt get there?

How can it be extracted without the need to dig mines?

The website http://www.lionsaltworkstrust.co.uk/making.htm is useful for this research.

How can we get salt from the sea?

We cannot drink sea water or use it to water crops. How can we turn sea water into fresh water?

The website http://www.ga.usgs.gov/edu/drinkseawater.html gives valuable information which can help with this research.

Problem solving

Once the children have been introduced to the basic concepts within this area of the National Curriculum, it is possible to extend their thought processes by problem solving. The permutations are many but here are some examples:

The head teacher's sugar has been spilt in the sandpit and she wants it back for her cup of coffee!

Iron filings have been spilt in the saltcellar.

Pupils can devise their own methods for separating all sorts of mixtures of solids, such as:

- sand, rice, dried peas and paper clips
- wooden beads, marbles and ball bearings (about the same size).

Who wrote the note?

There may have been a mysterious piece of writing and the author needs to be found. The author (conveniently) used a water-soluble felt-tip pen – this pen can be identified by using chromatography. Chromatography can be used to show whether a substance is pure or contains other substances (in this example by separating the dyes in the ink). It is achieved by placing a dot of ink on a strip of filter paper and dipping the end of the filter paper into a suitable solvent, in this case water. As the water travels across the filter paper the dyes, travelling at different rates, will be separated. The pattern produced on the filter paper is called a chromatogram. Ink from a variety of pens can be tested and the chromatograms compared with that produced by the ink used in the message.

The following website gives details about how to set up a simple chromatography experiment:

> http://sciencelessons.digitalbrain.com/digitalbrain/web/subjects/1.%20primary/ks2sci/su3/mod5/exercise2.db_psc?verb=view

The process can also be applied to coloured sweets:

> http://www.tki.org.nz/r/science/scienceschool/resources/physical/coloursinsweets_e.htm

Investigations

The factors that effect the rate at which solids dissolve in water can form the basis of a number of challenging investigations. The complexity of the investigation can be developed in a number of ways. In all of the investigations able children will be expected to decide how to carry out a fair test, decide what apparatus to use, make careful observations and measurements and make comparisons and draw conclusions.

What factors affect the solubility of salt in water?

This is a completely open investigation so the pupils are left to decide what they want to investigate and then plan accordingly.

How does the size of particles affect the rate that sugar dissolves in water?

Caster sugar and granulated sugar can be used and children need to time how long they take to dissolve. They will need to consider the variables that need to be controlled, such as the amount of stirring and the volume of water.

How long will it take for icing sugar to dissolve?

They can then predict how long they think that icing sugar will take to dissolve and carry out the investigation to test their prediction. They may expect the icing sugar to dissolve more quickly because the particles are smaller. In practice, they will find that icing sugar behaves differently and they can evaluate their findings accordingly. Icing sugar also contains an anti-caking agent, which forms a suspension in water. The sugar in it does dissolve but the resulting solution is cloudy because of this anti-caking agent.

How does the temperature of the water affect the time it takes sugar to dissolve?

The pupils will need to measure the temperature of the water and the time it takes for the sugar to dissolve. This gives the pupils the opportunity to work with continuous variables and so plot a line graph.

7 Sc4 Physical processes

Electricity

QCA units (DfEE/QCA 1998): 4F Circuits and conductors; 6G Changing circuits

Bright ideas

Why are insulators as important as conductors?

It is interesting to realise that electricity would be unusable if insulators did not exist, as well as conductors. Turning on any switch would be a shocking experience! This may be a good time to reinforce the dangers of mains electricity.

What would life be like without electricity?

This gives pupils the opportunity to make links with cross-curricular or topic work.

PMI

PMI: Consider the positives, minuses and interesting points associated with this scenario:

Having a computer chip implant which allows you to turn all electrical devices on by thinking about them.

Hot seating

You are Michael Faraday

Pupils can research this using books or the Internet and then be hot seated by the class.

Pupils as researchers

One of the best ways to teach electricity is by a structured discovery approach. This will allow the pupils to research the subject practically so that they try out electrical components to make up the circuits for themselves. Children tend to enjoy this approach and their level of engagement will be much higher if they are allowed to discover how to make a bulb light, rather than being shown how to make a circuit. When learning about electricity the emphasis should always be on practical activities and so it is vital that the school has sufficient equipment to allow this to take place.

It is possible to maintain structure in their learning by presenting them with a series of progressive challenges. A selection of such challenges are provided under the heading 'Practical electrical challenges'. They are not numbered so that appropriate ones can be picked out and presented to the pupils.

This is one of the times when it is beneficial to allow the more able to work together so that they can work through the challenges at their own pace. They can then be set one of the suggested problem-solving activities or develop their thinking further through an investigation linked to one of the challenges. It also allows for the curriculum to be compacted, as it is possible that the able children will have a clear understanding of the simpler challenges.

When asked to draw their circuit, if they have not yet met circuit diagrams, it is likely that they will produce an artistic representation of their circuit. It is then a good time to show them that it is possible draw the circuit in a way that other scientists will understand. Thus, they can be introduced to circuit diagrams. They may be a little angry that this takes you a few seconds to draw, whereas it took them considerably longer but they will certainly understand the value of such diagrams.

It is not required for the pupils to be introduced to parallel circuits at Key Stage 2, but it is inevitable that they will come across them when this type of research approach is used. It is probably best to explain that this is a special type of circuit, which produces some unusual results, such as the brightness of two bulbs and a battery being identical to the brightness of just one bulb and the same battery.

Practical electrical challenges

- Given a battery, wires and a bulb in a holder, make the bulb light.
- Make a bulb light and then draw your circuit so that you will remember how you did this.
- Make the bulb light outside the holder.
- Design a circuit which will test out which materials allow electricity to flow through them. Take this tester around the classroom and try out as many materials as possible.
- Make more than one bulb light from the one battery.
- Try out the other components, such as motors and buzzers.
- Construct a switch, something which can be pushed or moved so that the electricity is turned on or off.
- Construct as many different types of switches as possible.
- Find out what happens to the brightness of bulbs when more than one is added to a circuit.

- Find out if the length of the wires in a circuit makes any difference to the brightness of a bulb.
- In pairs, make circuit diagrams for each other and predict the brightness of the bulb/s in the circuits you have drawn. Set up the circuits that your partner has drawn to find out if they were right.

Theoretical research challenges

While electricity should be mostly practical, research that links to real life also has value and can be used to add breadth. Search engines such as http://www.yahooligans.com will provide suitable links for the following research suggestions:

Electricity in the body – Find out about the use of a pacemaker, electrocardiographs (ECGs), brain function.

How is electricity made?

Find out about renewable and non-renewable energy sources.

Find out about 'electric' animals, for example the electric eel.

Problem solving

Once the basic skills have been grasped, the subject of electricity lends itself particularly well to problem solving as a way of providing challenge. This is so open-ended that it can be used with the whole class. Ideally, the problem is best related to a real life situation and requires the pupils to draw on their existing scientific knowledge.

The pupils will need the electricity equipment and junk modelling materials, such as boxes, tubes, kitchen foil, card etc. Aluminium foil (cooking foil), bare copper wire and insulated wire that can be stripped to make connections are also useful.

Some suggestions are provided here but there are endless possible variations. With imagination, the problem can be linked to topic work or the season.

Hamster in danger!

Wire up the cage so that an alarm is raised if anyone opens the door.

To save the hamster from too much stress, the pupils can be encouraged to make a mock cage from a shoe box for the testing of their designs.

Protect my lunch box!

There may be someone who has a particular liking for chocolate biscuits so that people's lunch boxes are in danger. Ask the pupils to make an alarm system so that a warning is raised if a lunch box is moved. A box can be used as a mock lunch box.

Protect the school jewels!

The pupils are asked to design a burglar alarm that operates when a door is opened. There is more challenge in making an alarm come on when a door is opened, rather than when a door is closed. Another variation on this is looking at fridge doors and seeing if the pupils can design a mock fridge whose light comes on when the door is opened. They can then look at working fridges and compare mechanisms.

Make a dimmer switch

Pupils are asked to design a switch that gradually increases the brightness of a bulb (a dimmer switch) or can quickly turn it off. The inside of a pencil is made of graphite and if it is stripped and connected at different points, it will act as a dimmer. Fuse wire wrapped around a dowelling rod also makes an effective dimmer switch.

Make a remote-controlled car

The pupils are asked to design a model vehicle that is driven by an electric motor, using a belt drive. The car can be made of Lego Technic, possibly in design and technology. It is possible to purchase (cheaply) components that fit on the drive shaft of electric motors so that an elastic band can link the motor to an axle of a car. It is quite a challenge to design the car so that the motor is secure and the tension in the elastic band is such that the car moves at a sensible speed.

Pupils can then devise a switch, which allows the vehicle to move forwards or backwards. They can also make lights that flash on and off.

Investigations

What factors affect the brightness of a bulb?

This question encourages a completely open investigation, which will provide considerable challenge. The focus is on investigating factors which affect the brightness of bulbs – what changes will make the bulb brighter or dimmer?

The emphasis will be on making predictions, fair testing, interpreting patterns and drawing simple conclusions that show a link between cause and effect. To challenge the pupils even further they can be asked to devise a method for measuring brightness (for example, the number of pieces of paper needed to block the light out). This will give quantitative data which will allow the pupils to draw graphs from their results and look for patterns in their data.

Some pupils will need more support and so the more closed question, 'Examine the effect of different batteries or bulbs', may be more appropriate for them. This will mean that the whole class can be involved in similar, but differentiated, work.

Forces and motion

QCA units (DfEE/QCA 1998): 3E Magnets and springs; 4E Friction; 5C Gases around us; 6E Forces in action

Bright ideas

Gravity

Introduce the topic of gravity using the question below and an illustration such as Figure 7.1.

Figure 7.1 Why don't Australians drop off?

Why don't Australians drop off?

In response to this question, the pupils are more than likely to say that it is because of gravity and think that this then explains all.

The National Curriculum states that pupils need to understand that objects are pulled downwards because of the gravitational attraction between them and the Earth. The following question will encourage pupils to probe this further.

What is gravity and what causes it?

Very often this question prompts such replies as:

'Magnetism.'
'The spin of the Earth.'
'The atmosphere pushing down on objects.'

In fact, none of these answers has anything to do with gravity at all. It is a good question because scientists are not sure what causes gravity and so pupils can begin to appreciate that all is not cut and dried – there is still plenty that needs to be understood.

What is known is that gravity is a force that exists between all masses. Mass is measured in kilograms and is just the amount of matter in a body. Mass attracts mass. This does not seem at all logical because we do not feel a force of attraction when we walk past another person. At least, we cannot use this as an excuse to fall into their arms! It appears to be counter-intuitive. In fact, the reason we do not feel this force is because it is so small. However, the size of the force increases as the size of one or both of the masses increases. Hence I do not feel the force of attraction between me and another person but I do feel the force between myself and the Earth, because the Earth has a very large mass. The force that I feel between myself and the Earth is my weight, which is the pull I experience in Newtons towards the centre of the Earth.

Once the previous discussion has been held, the pupils know enough to be able to reason out an answer to this big question:

Why do people weigh less on the Moon?

The astronauts who landed on the Moon were highly educated, serious men. However, photographs show that when they landed, they bounced like Tigger! This was because they were enjoying the experience of weighing less. It is not uncommon for people to think that there is no gravity on the Moon. There is gravity but the pull is less than on Earth.

The astronauts weighed less on the Moon because the mass of the Moon is so much smaller than that of the Earth. The size of the force of attraction (gravity) depends on the size of the two masses being attracted to each other. If I travelled to the Moon my mass would not change, but the mass of the Moon is less than the mass of the Earth, so the pull I would feel to the centre of the Moon is less than the pull I feel towards the centre of the Earth. The astronauts weighed less on the Moon, i.e. the pull downwards was less, and so their muscles could make them jump considerably higher on the Moon than on the Earth.

If I went to a planet which had a greater mass than the Earth, I would weigh more and so I would find it harder to jump because of the relatively greater gravitational pull.

This discussion can lead to another big question:

Earthlings travel to different planets to take place in an Olympic games.

What do you think will happen?

Supposing that humans travel to each of the planets to take place in an Olympic games. Each event will take place simultaneously on all the different planets and the TV pictures relayed to decide the winner. What is likely to be the outcome?

The results will depend on the mass of each of the planets. If a planet has less mass than the Earth, then the contestants will weigh less and so are likely to fare much better in the weightlifting and high jump than those taking part on planets with a greater mass.

Friction

Discussion about friction as a force, which slows moving objects or may prevent movement, can also provide ideas for challenging children's ideas and thinking.

PMI: Consider the positives, minuses and interesting points associated with:

A world where there is no friction.

Friction is a force that slows moving things down and so it has a huge effect on life. If there was no friction cars would need to use far less fuel because, once they have started moving, there would be nothing to stop them. However, friction can be helpful and it allows us to keep a grip when walking, so life in a world with no friction would be rather precarious. Pedestrians would be falling everywhere and cars would not be able to grip the road at corners.

PMI: Consider the positives, minuses and interesting points associated with:

Water being as thick as treacle.

It would be very difficult to make a decent cup of tea and as for swimming . . . Ships would need to use far more fuel to cope with the increased resistance as they move through the water.

Pupils as researchers

There are a number of different aspects of forces that can form the basis of research activities for able pupils. For example:

At the bottom of steep hills, there are escape tracks. Carry out research into why they are there, what they are made from and how they work.

Gravel usually forms the surface of an escape track and it is positioned so that, if a car's brakes fail on a steep hill, the driver can direct it into this track. The friction caused by the car moving over the gravel is large and, hopefully, the car will come to rest quickly and safely. The following website has more details:

http://www.usroads.com/journals/rej/9708/re970801.htm

Research topics and related websites

- The 'Grav Lab' on the website http://library.thinkquest.org/27585/provides a number of different experiments for children to experiment with different aspects of gravity.
- On the website http://www.sodaplay.com children can examine and build virtual wire frame models. Once the models are built they can be tested under different force conditions, for example changing friction, gravity and tension.

Problem solving

All aspects of forces lend themselves to the development of problem-solving activities, for example magnets, friction, gravity, measuring forces and structures.

Magnets

It is a good idea to have some quite strong magnets so that the pupils can really feel the force of repulsion. Magnets will lose their magnetism when continually dropped so some replacements may be necessary. As an adult, Einstein remembered the awe he sensed when he first played with magnets so encourage the pupils to enjoy investigating pairs of magnets.

There are two identical looking bars: one is a magnet and the other is made of a material that is attracted to a magnet. Devise a means of finding out which is which. Explain your method.

It is possible to differentiate the two bars simply by putting a paper clip next to each one. The clip will only be attracted to the magnet. Alternatively, another magnet can be used. This magnet will experience a force of attraction with one end of the bar which is a magnet and repulsion with the other end, but with the other bar it will only experience a force of attraction towards the magnetic material.

Friction

Design, make and test as many different ways as you can to move a heavy object.

This can be linked with work, for example, on the ancient Egyptians and the pupils can hypothesise as to how the huge blocks were moved to the site of the pyramids. Another, related puzzle is the building of Stonehenge. They can experiment with a brick and the ways of moving the brick might include lifting, dragging, using a sledge, or runners and rollers. It may involve making a boat and moving it on water. The important thing is to encourage innovation and fair testing.

Gravity

Design and make a parachute that allows a 5 g mass to fall as slowly as possible from a height of 2 m.

This challenge will encourage the pupils to consider the factors that make for the slowest descent. It will also be interesting for them to consider a situation where the aim is for something to go slower, rather than faster.

The website http://www.paperairplanes.co.uk has a number of designs for paper aeroplanes and a spinner. Children can choose from them or develop their own ideas for the following challenges.

Design a spinner that falls 2 m in a set time, for example 4 seconds.

Competition time

Design a paper aeroplane that can stay in the air the longest.

Measuring forces

As we increase the force on an elastic band, it stretches further. This information can be used to challenge children by setting them the problem:

How can you use an elastic band to measure the weight of different objects?

In order to achieve this, the pupils will need to make and calibrate a measuring instrument. In other words, they will need to use a known weight, such as 100 g and find out how much this stretches an elastic band. They can then add weights and measure the stretch each time. A line graph of stretch against weight can be plotted. When an unknown weight is added they can measure the stretch and use the graph to find the weight.

Structures

The pupils are given a limited number of Art straws and some Sellotape and are then set one of the following challenges:

Build the highest tower that supports a mass of 25 g.

Build the strongest bridge across a 20 cm gap.

Investigations

Many of the problem-solving activities already described can be adapted to form science investigations.

The wobbly parachute problem

When parachutes were first made, it was discovered that, as they fall, they wobble and swing from side to side. Putting a hole in the top of the parachute cured this problem. The pupils can be asked to investigate the effects of a hole in a parachute. Introducing the investigation in the historical context of it being a real-life problem tends to encourage motivation and engagement. They can measure the time it takes for a parachute to fall with holes of different sizes. They can be encouraged to make predictions before carrying out their fair tests. They should be able to examine the data that they obtain for patterns and draw appropriate conclusions.

What makes the best spinner?

Investigating paper spinners is an activity found in unit 6E (Forces in action) of the QCA Scheme of Work. The able pupils can be guided to focus on continuous variables in their investigations such as the mass on the spinner or the length of the wings. This will give the children data that can be used to draw a line graph. A further focus can be on the accuracy of measurements made and the need to carry out more than one test. This will give children data from which to work out averages. They will have to decide if the mean, median or mode is the best one to use. The website http://www.paperairplanes.co.uk provides instructions for making spinners and paper planes.

> **Which shapes make moving through water the easiest?**
>
> The shape of bodies is important to animals that live in the water and streamlining is an advantage. The investigation can be carried out by dropping different shapes through a column of water and timing their descent or by dragging shapes through water.

Cars and ramps

There are a number of investigations that pupils can carry out when rolling things down ramps. For example, rolling balls of plasticine of different sizes, model cars of different weights and changing the height of the ramp. All involve continuous variables, which will allow children to collect data that can be used to draw line graphs.

Magnets

Pupils are given a selection of magnets and asked:

> **Which magnet is the strongest?**
>
> Pupils will devise their own investigation after examining the magnets and making predictions. Ideas can include the number of paper clips picked up, the thickness of material that the magnet will attract a paper clip through or the distance away from the magnet that an object is attracted (i.e. the further away it is attracted the stronger the magnet). If strong bar magnets are available, the children can extend the investigation further by examining which is the strongest part of a magnet. This can be carried out by marking 1 cm spaces along the magnet and finding out how long a chain of small paper clips can be attracted to each section. As always, the pupils should be asked to come up with their own plan for the investigation.

Light

QCA units (DfEE/QCA 1998): 3F Light and shadows; 6F How we see things

Bright ideas

The fact that darkness is the absence of light is a big idea. It is rare to be in a situation where it is completely dark. Children, particularly, tend to like to be able to see a light and so landing lights are left on outside bedrooms at night or streetlights shine through the curtains. It is often during caving expeditions at outdoor pursuit centres that children first experience total darkness. If it is likely that some of the children have experienced this, then the science can be explored as follows:

What is it like when there is absolutely no light?

Being in pitch darkness, where a hand literally cannot be seen in front of a face, brings home the concept that there needs to be a source of light in order to see.

Then, of course, the bigger question is:

Why is it like this?

As Hollins and Whitby (1998) point out, when children first accept the presence of light it is 'just there' and they tend not to understand that it travels from a source. Light travels so quickly that this is actually a very hard concept to grasp. Many pupils have a 'person-centred' view of light, in other words we see because we look and light just helps. The concept of seeing because light travels into the eye and that this light comes from a source requires some deep thinking.

Throwing a ball across the room and seeing that it takes time to go from one side of the room to the other may help them grasp the concept that light also takes time to travel. The night sky can be used to develop this huge idea. Light travels faster than anything else we know but the objects in the night sky are very, very far away. Light from the Sun takes eight and a half minutes to reach us. Light from the nearest star takes just over four years and light from other visible stars can take anything up to two million years to reach us.

Having being told these facts, the pupils can discuss the following fact:

The light that comes to my eye now from a distant star left that star millions of years ago. That means that we see history every night.

We see the stars as they were when the light left them. This means that there is a chance that some of the stars that we see no longer exist. Since the light that enters our eyes left them thousands or millions of years ago, it is possible that some have undergone a catastrophic happening and no longer exist as stars. It is also salutary to consider the fact that when the light left some of these stars, dinosaurs existed on Earth. The light that enters our eyes from these stars has been travelling in space since the time of the dinosaurs.

The programmes of study state that children need to understand about the formation of shadows. Children can be given Keogh and Naylor's concept cartoon 12.8 'Two Trees' (Naylor and Keogh 2000) to consider the concept of shadows more fully.

What is different about what we see when it is nearly dark and what we see when we are in bright light?

When it is fairly dark, we see in black and shades of grey. We only see colours when there is enough light. Our eyes are remarkable organs and there are two types of cells in the eye that detect light: rods and cones. The cones only work in bright light and they detect colour. The rods need far less light but they do not detect colour. The pupils may also be aware that our eyes 'dark adapt'. In other words, the longer that we stay in the dark, the more that we can see as our eyes become accustomed to the dark. However, if there is no light at all then we will see nothing.

PMI: Consider the positives, minuses and interesting points associated with the scenario that:

Our eyes only see in black and white.

If rods and cones have been discussed, the previous scenario can be reworded as:

Our eyes evolved so that they only have rods and do not have any cones.

Investigations

Which are the best sunglasses?

This can take the form of a consumer test where children collect information about preferences on designs but more fundamentally it is an investigation which is ideally suited to the use of light sensors connected to a computer. It is then possible to see how much light each pair of sunglasses will allow through.

If a pair of eclipse glasses is included these let no light through but of course we cannot see through them either which makes walking an issue! Shining light through the glasses and measuring the amount that has emerged using the sensor will allow the children to draw graphs from their data. The investigation can be changed and contextualised if the children are studying the Second World War. They can then investigate which material makes the best blackout curtains.

What affects the size of a shadow?

This is a very open investigation, which gives children the opportunity to use continuous variables. The investigation can examine the effect on the height of the shadow when the distance of the object from the screen is changed. Alternatively, the distance the light is from the object can be changed. Both of these investigations will give data that can be displayed using line graphs.

Pupils as researchers

Light linked to the ability to see and be seen can be an exciting topic for children to research. Some areas of interest include:

Animals that give out natural light in the form of bioluminescence.

How do animals that live under the ground cope in an environment without light?

Problem solving

Design and make a shadow clock – a sundial

Shadows from the sun move round as the sun 'moves' across the sky. The shadow length will also change, as the sun gets higher and then lower in the sky. The problem can be set without any initial discussion about the movement of the sun to allow children to use previous knowledge and understanding to develop their ideas. The challenge is for them to set up a sundial so that they can tell the approximate time – weather permitting.

Sound

QCA unit (DfEE/QCA 1998): 5F Changing sounds

Bright ideas

How does a 'silent' dog whistle work?

The pitch is too high for the human ear to detect but a dog's hearing will pick it up.

PMI: Consider the positives, minuses and interesting points associated with the following scenarios:

Having super sensitive hearing

An ear in the middle of your hand

Which is the odd one out?

- A recorder, an oboe and a trumpet
- A guitar, a harpsichord and a violin

This exercise may provide an incentive for the pupils to undertake some research to find out more about these different instruments.

Pupils as researchers

Investigate the school's musical instruments

For each instrument pupils will need to decide:

- What is vibrating?
- How does the design of the instrument enhance the sound?
- How is the note changed?

Stringed instruments have soundboxes, such as the hole behind the strings of an acoustic guitar which increases the volume of air vibrating.

Design and make musical instruments

If different groups are given types of instruments to design and make, such as percussion, stringed and wind then a class orchestra could result. The more able will be expected to carefully consider the design, which may include a soundbox and/or some means of changing the pitch of the note.

How do your ears work?

The human ear is a wonderful organ and provides a very suitable topic for research. ENCARTA (Microsoft 2000) has a good animation of the sound waves reaching the ear which shows the amazing mechanisms for the transmission of the vibrations.

Investigate acoustics

The reflection of sound is responsible for the acoustics of a room. A person's voice sounds very different if they are speaking in a cathedral or a sports hall, where there are many flat surfaces, than if they are speaking in a well-carpeted and curtained lounge. The sound of the person's voice bounces off the surfaces of the room and combines with the original sound and so if there are many echoes, the sound is prolonged. Similarly, if a person speaks in the middle of a field, their voice can sound very flat because there are no reflections. The pupils can make recordings such as these and then play them to the rest of the class and see if any difference can be spotted.

Ancient cathedrals used to have open pots set into the walls to improve the acoustics and modern concert halls have ceilings that move and different surfaces that can be raised and lowered to alter the acoustics. This is an interesting area for pupils to research.

Investigations

Sound needs something to travel in and this can be air but it can also be other media. It is fun to tie a piece of string to a teaspoon and to hold the string to your ear. If the spoon is allowed to dangle from the string and is made to knock into a hard surface, such as a desk, then it is surprising how loud this sounds in your ear. A string telephone works in a similar manner and they can be used as the basis for a very informal and open investigation.

Investigate string telephones

String telephones can be made very easily from yoghurt pots and string. The pupils can, for example, investigate how changing the length of the string affects the sound heard. They can, for example, change the yoghurt pots for other containers or change the thickness of the string. Is it possible to have a three-way conversation?

In the above example, it is only really possible to measure the effect on the sound subjectively. However, if the school has a sound sensor linked to a computer available there are a number of interesting quantitative investigations that can be developed:

Tell the story of the graph

With portable data-logging equipment, it is possible to leave a sound sensor running in, for example, the classroom from the end of the school day and throughout the night. The next morning the data can be downloaded onto a computer and a graph plotted. Interpreting a graph can then be both exciting and challenging. The noise level will drop as the pupils leave but then may rise again as tired teachers recap their eventful day. Who knows what will happen to the noise level overnight? Each pupil can have a copy of the graph and write the story in note form under the line graph. This will encourage them to use their imagination as to why the noise levels fluctuated and also clarify their understanding of graphs. They can then suggest other possible situations where the use of logging of sound levels may be interesting.

Cut noise pollution!

Pupils can investigate muffling sound using different materials or layers of material. A source of sound, such as an electric buzzer, can be contained in a tin and the layers of material wrapped around this. The data from the sensor will allow them to draw a bar chart from their results. They will make predictions, decide what source of sound to use and make sure the test is fair.

Earth and beyond

QCA unit (DfEE/QCA 1998): 5E Earth, Sun and Moon

Bright ideas

The big question as to how the pupils know that the Earth really is a sphere is given in Chapter 2. The National Curriculum also requires the pupils to

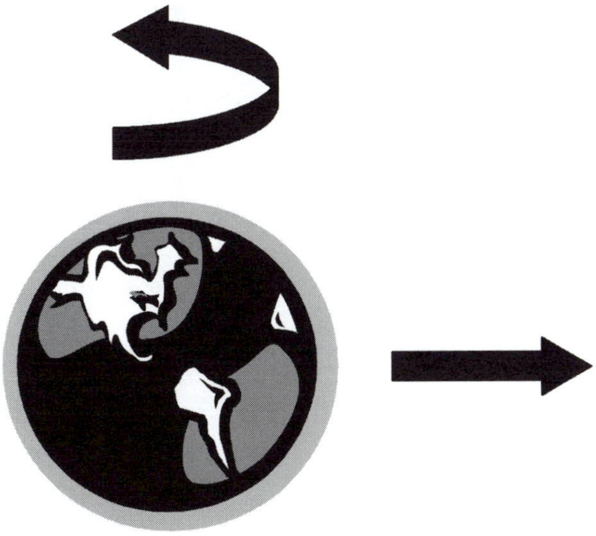

Figure 7.2 The Earth spins on its own axis and revolves around the Sun – why don't we feel dizzy?

relate the spin of the Earth to day and night and to understand that the Earth orbits the Sun once a year. Now this is a great deal of motion. We are inhabitants of an Earth that is spinning on its own axis and revolving around the Sun (Figure 7.2). This begs the question:

Why don't we feel dizzy?

We are expected to believe that all this motion is going on and yet we feel nothing. Why not?

This was, of course, one of the problems for poor Galileo in the seventeenth century, when he put forward his idea that the Earth rotates around the Sun, rather than the then accepted idea that the Sun rotates around the Earth. It is equally interesting to ask adults the same question. Their responses are often similar to children's and a common reply is, 'We are moving so slowly that we cannot feel it.'

Now if the size of the Earth is considered and the fact that it turns all the way around once every 24 hours, then it cannot be moving slowly – in fact, quite the reverse. The Earth is also moving on a huge orbit around the Sun once a year so it is, in fact, moving very fast indeed. The fact is that everything is moving with us and so we do not sense the motion. It is rather like being on a ship at night in a very calm sea – we would only sense the motion if the ship altered its speed.

Hidden behind the Earth and beyond curriculum then are some huge concepts and questions, but none more so than the awesome scale of the universe. It is almost impossible to grasp the meaning of these numbers and to get a feel for the scale involved. A useful demonstration is that of two small beads hanging by threads from a rod (Figure 7.3). One bead represents the Earth and the other the Moon. One bead should be slightly larger than the other and they need to be about 10 cm apart. Children can then be shown a variety of possible models for the Sun on the same scale: a golf ball, a tennis ball, a football and, finally, a large beach ball. They can then decide which would be about right for the relative size of the Sun – the answer is the large beach ball.

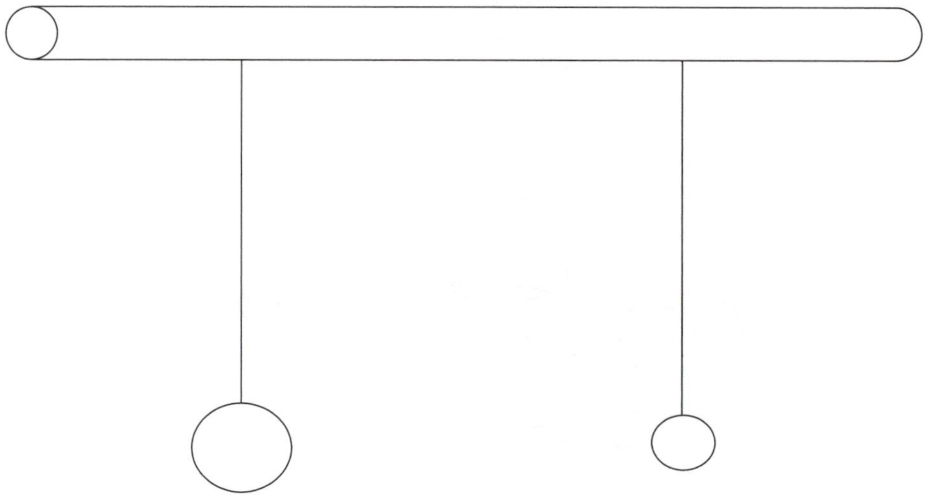

Figure 7.3 Model of the Earth's size and position relative to that of the Moon

This gives an idea of how much bigger the Sun is than the Moon. It is therefore absolutely amazing that the Moon and the Sun appear to be just about identical in size when viewed from Earth.

> **Why do the Sun and the Moon look the same size in the sky?**
>
> The Sun appears the same size as the Moon because it is much further away. In fact, the diameter of the Sun is 400 times the diameter of the Moon but it is also 400 times further away. This is an amazing coincidence which means that the disc of the Sun, as we see it from the Earth, is almost identical in size to the disc of the Moon in the sky. The Moon can therefore just cover the Sun and obscure it completely during a total eclipse.

> **How far away does the beach ball Sun need to be on this scale?**
>
> It can be thrown to the middle of the class, back of the class etc. but this would not be far enough – it needs to be 40 m away! At this distance, the large beach ball will seem to be the same size as the small bead representing the Moon.

Having presented this model, it is also interesting to ask the children:

> **What is between the Earth and the Sun?**
>
> Admittedly, there are two other planets between them but these are also relatively tiny (pea-like) and are in constant orbit around the Sun. Children tend to have quite a crowded picture of space and tend to think that there are other stars between the Earth and the Sun. They may also mention meteorites, asteroids etc. They will be very small amounts of matter but basically, there is just about nothing between the Sun and us. Nothingness is a very difficult concept to grasp.

Holding up the beads on the string and emphasising the scale again and the fact that the beach ball Sun is 40 m away ask the question:

> **Where would the next star be to our Sun?**
>
> Incredibly, on this same scale with the Sun 40 m away from the Earth, the nearest star would be 4000 km away! So if the bead model is held up in a room in central England, the model Sun is 40 m away on the same scale, and the nearest star would need to be on the west coast of Canada. This is undoubtedly awesome and particularly so when it is remembered that this is the position of our nearest, neighbouring star. This is just over four light years away and the majority of stars are far, far further away.

Pupils as researchers

The Earth and beyond is a natural topic for children to be given to research. There is a wealth of information available in textbooks, CD-ROMs and on the Internet. Children's astronomy books are often sold in the bargain bookstores and provide a valuable resource for research. The Hubble telescope (http://www.stsci.edu/) provides beautiful pictures and useful information.

By entering the NASA website (http://www.nasa.gov), a wealth of exciting information can be found and up-to-the-minute space news becomes available.

Prepare a foreign correspondent's report from Mars

It is not usually a good idea to ask pupils just 'to do some research' and it is preferable to give their work a focus. In order to prepare a foreign correspondent's report they will need to research the planet and they can be encouraged to report, for example, on how it would feel on its surface: Will they feel heavy or light? Will they be able to breathe? How many moons can be seen in the sky? What colour is the sky?

References

Adey, P. and Shayer, M. (1994) Really Raising Standards: Cognitive intervention and academic achievement. London: Routledge.

Allebone, B. (1998) 'Providing for able children in the primary classroom', *Education 3–13* March 1998, 64–9.

Assessment Reform Group (1999) *Assessment for Learning: Beyond the black box.* Cambridge: Cambridge University Press.

Black, P. and Wiliam, D. (1998) *Inside the Black Box.* London: King's College.

Bloom, B. (ed.) (1956) *Taxonomy of Educational Objectives Vol 1.* Harlow: Longman.

Cheshire County Council (2002) *Thinking Skills.* http://www.salt.cheshire.org.uk/MFL/thinking/intro.htm Accessed September 2002.

Clark, C. and Callow, F. (1998) *Educating Able Pupils.* London: David Fulton Publishers.

Coates, D. and Eyre, D. (1999) 'Can encouraging the use of higher order thinking skills in science help young able children achieve more highly?' paper prepared for the fourth Summer Conference for Teacher Education in Primary Science, University of Durham, July.

Coates, D. and Wilson, H. (2000) 'Science masterclasses for able children in Year 2', in McKeon, F. (ed.) *SCICentre 2000 and ASET Conference Report,* 101–7. Leicester: SCICentre, University of Leicester.

Coates, D. and Wilson, H. (2001) 'Science', in Eyre, D. and McClure, L. (eds) *Curriculum Provision for the Gifted and Talented in the Primary School.* London: David Fulton Publishers.

Csikszentmihalyi, M. (1990) *Flow: The psychology of optimal experience.* New York: Harper and Row.

Davis, G. A. and Rimm, S. B. (1998) *Education of the Gifted and Talented.* London: Allyn and Bacon.

De Bono, E. (1986) *Six Thinking Hats.* Harmondsworth: Viking.

Dennis, M. (2002) 'Have we got science for you', *Primary Science Review* **71**, 13–15.

Diezmann, C. M. and Watters, J. J. (2000) 'An enrichment policy and strategy for empowering young gifted children to become autonomous learners', *Gifted and Talented International* **XV**(1), Spring, 6–18.

DfEE/QCA (1998) *Science. A Scheme of Work for Key Stage 1 and 2.* London: QCA/DfEE.

DfEE/QCA (1999) *The National Curriculum. Handbook for primary teachers in England*. London: DfEE/QCA.

DfES (2002) *Schools Achieving Success*. http://www.dfes.gov.uk/achievingsuccess Accessed November 2002.

Dudley LEA (1998) *Meeting the Needs of the More Able Pupil*. Dudley: Dudley Publication.

Eyre, D. (1997) *Able Children in Ordinary Schools*. London: David Fulton Publishers.

Eyre, D. (2002) *Structured Tinkering: Improving provisions for the gifted in ordinary schools*. http://www.warwick.ac.uk/gifted/EZLstructured.htm Accessed January 2003.

Feasey, R., Goldsworthy, A., Phipps, R. and Stringer, J. (2001) *New STAR Science Series*. Oxford: Ginn.

Fisher, R. (1990) *Teaching Children to Think*. Cheltenham: Stanley Thorne.

Fisher, R. (1995) *Teaching Children to Learn*. Cheltenham: Stanley Thorne.

Freeman, J. (1991) *Gifted Children Growing Up*. London: Cassell.

Freeman, J. (1998) *Educating the Very Able: Current international research*. London: HMSO.

Gallagher, J. J. (1985) *Teaching the Gifted Child*. Newton: Allyn and Bacon.

Gardner, H. (1993) *Creating Minds: An anatomy of creativity seen through the lives of Freud, Einstein, Picasso, Stravinsky, Eliot, Graham and Gandhi*. New York: Basic Books.

George, D. (1997) *The Challenge of the Able Child*. London: David Fulton Publishers.

Goldsworthy, A. and Feasey, R. (1997) *Making Sense of Primary Science Investigations*. Hatfield: Association for Science Education.

Goldsworthy, A. and Holmes, M. (1999) *Teach it! Do it! Let's get to it!* Hatfield: Association for Science Education.

Goldsworthy, A., Watson, J. R. and Wood-Robinson, V. (1999) *Investigations: Getting to grips with graphs*. Hatfield: Association for Science Education.

Goldsworthy, A., Watson, J. R. and Wood-Robinson, V. (2000a) *Investigations: Developing understanding*. Hatfield: Association for Science Education.

Goldsworthy, A., Watson, J. R. and Wood-Robinson, V. (2000b) *Targeted Learning*. Hatfield: Association for Science Education.

Harlen, W. (2001) 'Developing children's thinking in primary science', *Teaching Thinking* Autumn, 8–13.

Harrison, S. (2001) 'SATs and the QCA Standards Report', *Primary Science Review* **68**, 28–9.

Hollins, M. and Whitby, V. (1998) *Progression in Primary Science*. London: David Fulton Publishers.

House of Commons (1999) 'Highly able children', Education and Employment Committee, Third Report. London: HMSO.

Hymer, B. and Michel, D. (2002) *Gifted and Talented Learners. Creating a policy for inclusion*. London: David Fulton Publishers.

Johnson, D., Boyce, L. and Van Tassel-Baska, J. (1995) 'Evaluating curriculum materials in science', *Gifted Child Quarterly* **89(**1), 35–43.

Jones, A. T., Simon, S. A., Black, P. J., Fairbrother, R. W. and Watson, J. R. (1992)

Open Work in Science. Development of investigations in schools. OPEN Project. King's College London: Association for Science Education.

Kerry, T. (1981) *Teaching Bright Pupils in Mixed Ability Classes.* Basingstoke: MacMillan Education.

Kerry, T. and Kerry, C. (2000) 'The centrality of teaching skills improving able pupil education', *Educating Able Children* **4**(2), 13–19.

Lewin, R. H. (1999) 'The more able in design and technology – seeing the same as everyone else and thinking something different', *Educating Able Children,* Spring, 9–13.

Lewis, A. and Smith, D. (1993) 'Defining higher order thinking', *Theory into Practice* **32**(3), 131–7.

Luxford, H. (1997) 'Where do I go from here? An approach to planning for enrichment in primary science', *Journal of NACE* Spring Issue 1, 3–9.

McGuinness, C. (2000) 'ACTS: A methodology for enhancing thinking skills across the curriculum', *Teaching Thinking* **1**(2), 49–52.

Mackay, A. L. (1977) *The Harvest of a Quiet Eye.* London: Institute of Physics.

Maker, J. (1982) *Curriculum Development for the Gifted.* Rockville: Aspen Systems Corporation.

Maker, C. J. and Nielson, A. B. (1995) *Teaching Models in Education of the Gifted.* Texas: Pro-ed.

Montague-Smith, A. and Winstone, L. (1998) *Supporting Science and Technology: A handbook for those who assist in early years settings.* London: David Fulton Publishers.

Montgomery, D. (1990) *Children with Learning Difficulties.* London: Cassell.

Montgomery, D. (1996) *Educating Able Children.* London: Cassell.

Montgomery, D. (2001a) *Able Underachievers.* London: Whurr.

Montgomery, D. (2001b) 'Teaching the more able: An update' *Gifted Education International* **15** (3), 262–80.

Naylor, S. and Keogh, B. (2000) *Concept Cartoons in Science Education.* Sandbach: Millgate House Publishers.

O'Brien, P. (1998) *Teaching Scientifically Able Pupils in the Primary School.* Oxford: NACE.

Ofsted (1999) *Annual Report of HMCI 1997/1998.* London: HMSO.

Ofsted (2000) *Handbook for Inspecting Primary and Nursery Schools, with guidance on self-evaluation.* London: TSO.

Ofsted (2001) *Annual Report of HMCI 1999/2000.* London: HMSO.

Ofsted (2002) *Changing Schools: An evaluation of the effectiveness of transfer arrangements at age 11.* London: HMSO.

Porter, L. (1999) *Gifted Young Children.* Buckingham: Open University Press.

QCA (2000) *Standards at Key Stage 2, English, mathematics and science.* London: QCA.

QCA (2001a) *Guidance on Teaching Gifted and Talented Pupils.* http://www.nc.uk.net/gt/general/05_assessment.htm Accessed December 2002.

QCA (2001b) *Working with Gifted and Talented Children. Key Stages 1 and 2 English and mathematics.* London: QCA.

QCA (2001c) *Guidance on Teaching Gifted and Talented Pupils.* www.nc.uk.net/gt/science/index.htm Accessed January 2003.

QCA (2003) *Years 3 to 6: Assessment and reporting arrangements.* London: QCA.

Qualter, A. and Webb, G. (1996) 'Differentiated science teaching. A case study in complexity', *Education 3–13* October 1996, 37–47.

QCA/DfEE (1999) *Science. The National Curriculum for England.* London: QCA.

QCA/DfEE (2000) *A Scheme of Work for Key Stages 1 and 2. Science teacher's guide update.* Sudbury: QCA.

Renzulli, J. S. (1986) 'The three-ring conception of giftedness: A developmental model for creative productivity', in Sternberg, R. J. and Davidson, J. E. (eds) *Conceptions of Giftedness.* Cambridge, MA: Cambridge University Press.

Rogers, K. B. (1999) *Research Synthesis Regarding Gifted Education Provision.* http://www.nsagtc.org.au/info/articles/RogersResearchSynthesis.html Accessed May 2002.

Shore, B. M. (2000) 'Metacognition and flexibility: qualitative differences in how gifted children think', in Friedman, R. C. and Shore, B. M. (eds) *Talent Unfolding: Cognition and development.* Washington DC: American Psychological Association.

Sis, P. (1996) *Starry Messenger.* Bath: Barefoot Books.

Swartz, R. (2002) 'Assessing critical and creative thinking: Examples and issues', paper presented at the 10th International Conference on Thinking, Harrogate.

Van Tassel-Baska, J. (1998) *Planning Science Programs for High Ability Learners.* http://ericec.org/digest/e546.html Accessed April 2002.

Webster's Third New International Dictionary (1981) Chicago: Merrian-Webster.

What's the Big Idea? series (1997–9) London: Hodder and Stoughton.

Wood, D. J. (1991) 'Aspects of teaching and learning' in Light, P., Sheldon, S. and Woodhead, M. (eds) *Learning to Think.* London: Routledge in association with the Open University.

Index